Table of Contents

Introduction

The years from birth to six are a unique period of development. During these magical years, the brain is wide open for input and fully engaged in a self-guided structuring process. This offers a golden opportunity to make a major positive difference in children's lives. With the right approach, we can help children realize more of their true potential throughout their lifetimes. The materials and activities shown in this book are some of the most positive, productive experiences you can provide your child.

Children make positive strides in development when we support and encourage their brain development. This starts with things parents can do every day, starting on page 18. Young children are hands-on learners, so the next step is to provide quality learning materials in an encouraging environment. High quality learning materials are found in Montessori schools all over the world. Parents can make most of the learning materials in this book very inexpensively. As more parents take an active role in helping their children learn, the home is becoming a place where young children are finding materials and activities that support and encourage their development.

Read the first chapters, make a Practical Life or Sensorial material first, and get started on your home early learning adventure right away. I encourage you to read one or more of the books listed on page 55. Be positive, patient, and encouraging, and have fun!

"The most important period of life is not the age of university studies, but the first one, from birth to the age of six. For this is when man's intelligence itself, his greatest implement, is being formed."

Maria Montessori

Quick Start Guide

If you are eager to start right away, try the steps below. I used a variation of this process to start three new Montessori preschools.

1. Read pages 6 - 55. It won't take long, I promise. You will be better prepared by understanding these core concepts and practices.

2. Find a spot on a low shelf in your child's room or elsewhere where you can display a few learning materials. This will get you started. You can set up a larger set of shelves (p. 29-30) later.

3. Pick a **Practical Life** (p. 56) or **Sensorial** (p. 76) material. Suggestions are given on page 32. Gather the materials, involving your child in the process, including any shopping involved. Make sure the material has its own tray, bowl, or other attractive container to hold everything

4. Have your child lay out a floor rug or a plastic table mat as a work area. Let her carry the material carefully to the work area.

5. Give your child a brief demonstration of the material.

6. Let your child work with it as long as he likes.

7. When she is done, have your child reorganize the material nicely back into its container and carry it to a spot on a shelf you picked earlier. Tell your child, *"This is where we will keep this for you to use."*

Follow these steps with each new activity. Soon, you will need a set of low shelves in your child's room (p. 29-30). Display materials you make, along with those you buy, on your child's shelves. Your child will build up a selection of materials she is currently using, ready for independent use. Help your child keep his shelves and materials organized and clean at all times, ready for use.

Soon, you will have a great home preschool.

People will be asking you how you did it!

Your Preschooler's Amazing Brain

Most parents are amazed at how fast their young children develop. Many parents over the years asked me if I thought their child might be gifted. There is a good reason for this – they all are! From birth to around age six, children have marvelous capabilities for absorbing information from their environment, learning new things, and mastering basic life skills. Children the world over learn to walk, talk, think, perceive the world accurately, and master many life skills in their first years of life, on a fairly similar timeline. They accomplish this remarkable feat of development even if adults do not directly help them all that much.

By age six, children develop into people suited to live in the time, place, and culture in which they are born. Preschoolers learn multiple languages if they hear them spoken regularly. The child who seemingly just spoke her first words now sings. In a few years, unsteady steps and clutching hand grasps evolve to dancing, playing sports, and writing with a pencil. The personality in basic form at two has depth and complexity by five. In only five or six years, we send our baby out the door and off to school. How did all that happen so fast?

The Italian educator Maria Montessori called the force that guides children's early development the *Inner Teacher*. She saw that children's play is the outward expression of a universal inner desire to learn about the world and take their place in it. She observed that children spontaneously reach out to explore, experience, and understand. She said:

> *"We discovered that education is not something which the Teacher does, but that it is a natural process that develops spontaneously in the human being."*

> *"Education is a natural process carried out by the child, and is not acquired by listening to words but by experiences in the environment."*

After creating the first environment that she prepared specifically to support and optimize the development of little children, Montessori continued observing the children. She discovered that the outward movements and explorations the children conducted with the special learning materials she invented were only part of the story. The children also exhibited the ability to *concentrate their attention* for significant periods of time as they repeated using different materials. After these periods of focused concentration, Montessori saw that the children were calmer and happier. Any behavioral or emotional issues they had gradually receded as more confident, calm, positive, and well-adjusted children emerged. Montessori called this process *Normalization*. This observation became a core principle of her work. Montessori said:

"The first essential for the child's development is concentration. The child who concentrates is immensely happy."

"Normalization is the single most important result of our work"

Montessori came to believe that when a young child intensely concentrates on using an activity or material, major structural and organizational work is happening within the child's brain. Since this activity satisfies the child's need to grow and develop, the child becomes calmer and happier. When we are hungry, we are agitated. Once fed, we calm down. Montessori saw that the children's self-guided explorations with learning materials were giving their brains the 'food' they needed to develop. In realizing this, Montessori discovered the main thing to remember about development in early childhood:

From birth to age 6, child development is all about the brain.

Modern neuroscience has discovered amazing things about brain development in young children. One of the best places to learn about this is at **developingchild.harvard.edu**, the web site of the **Center on the Developing Child at Harvard University**.

The human brain is a collection of nerves, or neurons. Each nerve has many branches that connect with the branches of other nerves. Brain nerves and their branches are pathways for electrical impulses. These impulses do the work of thinking, movement, and regulating our vital functions. Without nerves transmitting electrical impulses, there is no life. Nerve impulses travel the most freely during the first six years of life.

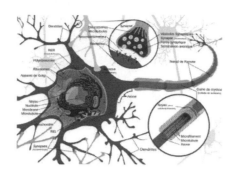

Drawing of a nerve

A baby has around 100 billion brain neurons at birth, or about the number of stars in the Milky Way Galaxy. The number of possible connections between the branches of these nerves numbers in the *trillions*. Every sense impression, movement, and thought sends electrical impulses racing through a child's brain from neuron to neuron. The pathways these impulses follow become brain circuits. Nerve circuits that are used frequently become very adept at transmitting impulses. They act like superhighways for electrical impulse transmission.

The first six years of a human life are a unique time when new brain nerve circuits are opened in huge numbers, with stunning speed. A young child opens as many as *700 new brain nerve pathways every second* for years. By around six years of age the cerebral cortex, or 'gray matter' of the brain, which controls sensory awareness, muscle control, language, thought, memory, problem solving, attention, awareness, visual recognition, and consciousness, has reached about 90% of its adult weight.

Every time your child moves a muscle, receives sensory impressions, thinks, speaks, acts intentionally, even dreams, electricity travels through her brain along nerve circuits. As a child uses brain circuits regularly, these pathways organize into a structural complex of nerve circuits which scientists call the **Brain Architecture**. This organized network of nerve pathways becomes the functional brain we use for the rest of our lives.

By six years of age, the foundational brain architecture we will use for life is in place. We have about six years from birth to help a child make fundamental positive changes in their brain architecture. The experiences a child has during those precious six years dramatically affect the quality and capability of the child's brain architecture. **From the Center on the Developing Child:**

> *"The quality of a child's early environment and the availability of appropriate experiences at the right stages of development are crucial in determining the strength or weakness of the brain's architecture."*

> *"The exceptionally strong influence of early experiences on brain architecture makes the early years of life a period of both great opportunity and great vulnerability for brain development."*

> *"Early experience has a unique advantage in shaping the architecture of developing brain circuits before they are fully mature and stabilized."*

> *"Early learning lays the foundation for later learning, and is essential for the development of optimized brain architecture."*

Around age six, another important brain process called **Brain Pruning** begins. The brain *eliminates* nerve pathways that have not been opened or have not been used frequently. Pruning reveals the essential brain architecture, just as the natural shape of a plant is seen after extraneous branches are pruned away. Knowing all this, we are at the same point Dr. Montessori was when she first observed this process. Montessori then asked a simple question:

> *"Can we **help life** as it unfolds from within the child?"*

Or today, we can ask:

> *"Can we help children build **stronger, more capable brain architecture** in their early years?"*

The answer is a definite yes. It is not hard to help your child develop a more capable, efficient brain. Parents can easily provide experiences that will build strong brain architecture in their children. In fact, they are some of the best people for doing this. You do not need a teaching degree, lengthy training, or an expensive preschool to help your child realize more of his true potential. This book will show you how and you can start right away.

Independence

"From the moment they are weaned, little children are making their way toward independence."

Montessori saw that young children have a strong desire to master the skills of daily life and become independent people. They are often frustrated in these efforts by adults who are afraid that children will make a mess, hurt themselves, or require enormous amounts of time to practice and learn these skills. Children of course make mistakes when they are learning. Montessori made a positive out of this, incorporating the cleaning up of spills into many of her materials and activities. Other materials have a built-in 'control of error', which makes it obvious to a child when an arrangement or layout needs to be changed, when the child is ready to see that. Montessori counseled teachers not to interfere to do things for a child, but to let him work things out on his own.

"It is well to cultivate a friendly feeling towards error, to treat it as a companion inseparable from our lives, as something having a purpose, which it truly has."

"Never help a child with a task at which he feels he can succeed."

A big part of doing early learning at home is giving your child the chance to practice and master the skills of daily living during your everyday life at home, and with the Practical Life materials (p. 56).

Movement

"Watching a child makes it obvious that the development of his mind comes through his movements. Since it is through movement that the will realizes itself, we should assist a child in his attempts to put his will into act."

Children simply have to move to develop properly. Movements build brain architecture, just as sensory impressions and thoughts do. Young children have a very close mind-body connection. As a child gradually acquires large and small muscle control and coordination, her mind is also becoming ordered and structured. There is a reason children are almost constantly in motion: movement is an essential element of their development.

You can support your child's need to move at home with large muscle activities such as exercise, yoga, dance, gymnastics, and free play outdoors; and with learning materials that promote small muscle development of the arms, hands, and fingers.

> *"The hands are the instruments of man's intelligence. The human hand allows the mind to reveal itself."*

Absorbent Mind

> *"Whereas an adult admires their environment, a child completely absorbs it. This absorption transforms the child and forms part of his or her soul."*

Montessori observed that young children, rather than learn fact-to-fact in a linear fashion, like adults, absorb information from all around them all at once, in a *global* way. She called this ability the **Absorbent Mind**. Modern neuroscience has shown that children continuously and readily accept an enormous number and wide variety of sensory inputs, all at the same time. They are soaking up everything about the world around them, which is why people sometimes call young children 'little sponges'.

Neuroscience has shown that the world we perceive is actually put together from a small fraction of the total number of sensory inputs we take in. It is in early childhood that we learn to pay attention to the same sensory inputs that older children and adults do. By about age 6, we have it down pat, and perceive the world pretty much like everyone else. Early learning materials help children refine and educate their senses and thinking skills, which facilitates this process.

> *"There is in a child a special kind of sensitivity which leads him to absorb everything about him; and it is this work of observing and absorbing that alone enables him to adapt himself to life."*

Sensitive Periods

Young children experience periods of time when they are especially interested in, and show an increased ability to learn about, various aspects of their environment. Montessori called these **Sensitive Periods**. Neuroscience has confirmed their existence:

"...specific experiences affect specific brain circuits during specific developmental stages – referred to as sensitive periods – it is vitally important to take advantage of these early opportunities in the developmental building process."

The Center on the Developing Child, Harvard University

There are sensitive periods for math, language, tiny objects, large muscle development, order and patterns, all kinds of things. Rather than try to identify or expectantly wait for your child to enter sensitive periods, it is perhaps better for parents to consider the **entire period from birth to six as one big sensitive period**. You will see soon enough when your child starts counting all the time and asking what written numbers and words mean. This is the time to start the **Math** and **Reading** sequences.

The learning materials in this book are your best friends when your child is really into something. If your child really likes the Transfers (p. 59), start with the water sponging transfer and progress according to your child's level of interest and her natural rate of muscle skills development. If it's math, start the **Math Sequence** (p. 131) and go as far as your child wants to go. The **Reading Sequence** (p. 152) will let you do the same with reading and writing. Having learning materials available means you will always have materials that match up with your child's current interests, and allow you to follow his interests as they change – and they will.

The Prepared Environment

After making her observations of children, Montessori could have written up a research paper and moved on to study something else. Thankfully, she followed through to find out the answer to the question, *"Can we help life as it unfolds from within the child?"*

To find out, Montessori created something totally new and very radical for the time – **an environment prepared and designed just for little children**. She created a beautiful, orderly space with many low shelves holding interesting, attractive, well-made materials the children could hold and manipulate. Everything was sized just for children – the first time anyone had ever done this! The children had freedom to choose what they wanted to work with, for how long, and whether to work alone or with others. This was the first **Montessori Prepared Environment**. It has now been duplicated, with modifications here and there, in Montessori preschools all over the world for over a century.

The learning materials and ideas in this book will help you bring many of the experiences children find in Montessori schools into your home. You will discover a new way to offer your child interesting things to do that meet her real developmental needs. Montessori is no longer the sole province of Montessori schools. Parents, as well as traditional preschool and day care operators, are finding that doing Montessori activities is easy and fun.

Montessori schools are known as places where young children learn to read, write, and develop mathematics skills at very young ages. In our schools, it was typical for a child who had attended at least 1-2 years from age 4-6 to be reading and writing at a second or third grade level, as measured by the standards used in public schools. This says more about the expectations public education has for students than it does about Montessori preschools.

Montessori education shows what is possible for children if they have the right environment, freedom to learn as nature intends, and encouragement. Montessori allows children to pursue their **natural passion for learning** from birth, and take it as far and as fast as they want to go. The fact that this leads children to significantly exceed the expectations of public education indicates that those expectations are too low. Let your child pursue the activities shown here in a spirit of fun and discovery, and she will surprise you. The Inner Teacher is a better motivator and guide than any adult-designed lesson plan. Follow your child and you will be surprised where things lead!

Helping Your Preschooler Build a Better Brain Every Day

Before we get into making fun learning materials, it is helpful to start using these basic principles in your parenting. These are core concepts you can put into action in your daily life before you begin making learning materials. All parents can do these things. These simple steps will start helping your child build strong brain architecture today.

Trust & respect your child's Inner Teacher

This means acknowledging that your child's play is her important work of growing up. Your child's activities and interests are meaningful and should be respected and encouraged.

> "We should respect all the reasonable forms of activity in which the child engages, and try to understand them."

We don't need lesson plans and schedules to structure a young child's learning. We present a consistently rich environment, trust the Inner Teacher, and observe our child for sparks of spontaneous focused attention. We provide more of whatever our child is into that moment, day, or week.

When speaking to your child, get on her eye level. Encourage him to tell you more by actively listening and acknowledging. Nod your head, be interested, and pay attention. Ask *open ended questions* rather than questions that elicit yes or no answers, like, *"Tell me more about that"*, *"How did that make you feel?"*, *"What did you think about that?"*, and *"What happened then?"*

In has become fashionable to praise children for everything they do and tell them constantly how smart and great they are. This really isn't necessary or even helpful. This is actually a misinterpretation of how to show respect for a child's journey of development. **Young children develop a positive self-image by mastering real skills and learning useful information**. This makes them feel competent and more in control of their environment.

We truly show children respect when we provide them with reasonable challenges to master, and then encourage their efforts. **Encouragement is preferred over praise** most of the time. Praise creates children who seek our approval for everything. It is fine to praise worthy achievements and special accomplishments. It is even more effective to encourage effort and perseverance in the face of challenges. *"You tried hard and did not give up, that's great!" "Everyone makes mistakes, keep trying, you'll get it."*

Create an orderly, attractive home environment

Young children absorb their environment. **Attractive, organized, aesthetically pleasing, clean environments help children internalize a sense of beauty and order.** What a child sees, handles, and interacts with every day becomes a part of her brain architecture.

You do not need to make your home a showplace fit for TV. Start by reducing clutter. De-clutter shelves and cabinets. Arrange furniture in pleasing ways. Keep things clean. Highlight surfaces with a few attractive, interesting items. Use a variety of materials, such as stone, natural textiles, plants, wood, metal, ceramics, and glass. A simple wooden or glass bowl half full of river rocks can be really interesting to a child. **Let your child touch**! Wooden, ceramic, and glass figures, bowls, and animals are great. Dry grasses and growing plants add an organic touch.

Display nice artwork in your home. Inexpensive fine art posters are available at *AllPosters.com*. Find inexpensive frames at *Displays2go.com*.

Take it outside with a simple brick or paver patio, a sandbox, a climbing structure, and an area for free play with objects like logs, rocks, dirt, pine cones, string, toy trucks, and people and animal figures.

Encourage Independence

Children want to be independent. They can do a lot if we take the time to show them how and let them practice. Teach your child how to do things he is capable of doing safely around the home at dinnertime, when cleaning up, and out in the yard. See what your child likes to do and do more of it.

Setting out plates and silverware, carrying things to the table, helping load the dishwasher, washing dishes, cleaning table tops and low shelves, pulling weeds, watering flowers with a watering can, folding clothes, learning to dress herself, pouring his own cereal, and properly washing hands are just a few of the many things children can learn to do. Every task or skill they master adds to a young child's self-confidence. See page 56.

Gaining independence in daily life starts a child on the road to becoming a self-motivated adult.

> *"Any child who is self-sufficient, who can tie his own shoes, dress and undress himself, reflects in his joy and sense of achievement the image of human dignity, which is derived from a sense of independence. The child's first instinct is to carry out his actions by himself, without anyone helping him, and his first conscious bid for independence is made when he defends himself against those who try to do the action for him."*

Maria Montessori

Use language creatively & constructively

Explain things to your child using correct speech and proper terms. Words have power. They are great brain stimulators. Correct terms will not be too difficult, children are simply absorbing language. They absorb proper terms and correct speech as easily as dumbed down speech and incorrect grammar. It's all a matter of what they are exposed to.

Use descriptive language to expand on observations and concepts. For example, instead of just saying, *"That is a pretty tree"*, you could say, as you touch the tree and point things out, *"Look at this beautiful strong tree. The trunk is straight and thick. The leaves are full and a deep shade of green. The bark is thick and rough. I'm sure this tree has strong roots that go deep into the ground. It must be at least twenty feet high."* Language like this gives your child new concepts and ideas to absorb, and opens many new brain nerve pathways. Get in the habit of looking up words you don't know online with your child. Build your vocabularies together. Write down new words and post them on the refrigerator.

Explain how things work. We forget what a mysterious place the world can be for a young child. Every time we help a child understand how something works and why something happens, we increase the child's knowledge and encourage his curiosity, while also opening more brain nerve pathways.

Ask open ended questions. Rather than ask questions that elicit yes or no answers, ask questions like, *"What do you think about that?"*, *"Why do you think that happens?"* and *"What does that make you think of?"* These questions make your child think, and encourage conversation and more use of language.

Actively listen to your child. Get eye to eye with your child. Look at her when she speaks and pay attention. Show you are listening by nodding your head and making facial expressions. Encourage her to speak with prompts such as, *"Really?"*, *"No kidding!"*, *"Is that right?"* *"Wow!"* Add in a few open ended questions.

Encourage movement

Young children have a highly integrated mind-body connection, and need plenty of muscle movement. They need to be outside playing, running, and climbing. Children need to dance, build, and exercise. **Movement builds strong brain architecture** in early childhood. Free play and exploration in nature is wonderful. There are programs for gymnastics, swimming, and soccer for young children in many areas. Every child should learn to swim around age 4. One of the great benefit of hands-on learning materials is the small muscle exercise and practice they provide. As a child gradually refines her grasp, she ideally becomes able to properly hold a pencil around the same time she is learning to write.

Play games

Children love board games and appropriate game apps. Good games teach information, logic, planning, strategy, and critical thinking. Children learn to take turns, and experience winning and losing.

Go places, do things, collect stuff, take photos and movies.

Expose your child to many different experiences. Children's brains are set on '*absorb*' all the time, and can handle lots of sensory input. Visit local fairs and gatherings, go to performances, walk around the city, and go to the top of a skyscraper. Get out in nature often. Visit playgrounds, parks, and national forests. Do art projects at home, and find places to bring your child into contact with other children in a positive way. You never know what experiences will 'stick' with a child and influence the course of his life.

Time in nature allows a child to absorb the rhythms of life outside the city. Collect interesting objects in a box or bag and bring them home to talk about later. Take photos and movies to relive your adventures. Print out photos and help your child make his own books about your trips. Memories open brain nerve pathways while filling the brain's memory banks.

Watch TV & internet videos together

My child should watch more video screens? If done in the right way, absolutely. Informative videos on You Tube are becoming primary teaching tools for young children. You can find wonderful short videos that are appropriate for preschoolers on almost any topic. There are many wonderful educational channels such as National Geographic, Nova, and the Discovery Channel. Plan ahead, control time and content, watch with your child, and discuss what you watch.

One study of the shared characteristics of families whose members rated their family life as satisfying listed watching TV together as a very positive activity. The key, as with many things in life, is balance.

Use consistent, positive discipline

Discipline comes from the Latin *disciplina*, which means teaching, learning, and knowledge. This nicely describes a positive, learning-based approach to helping a child learn new skills while developing an internal self-discipline.

By helping a child pursue her positive instincts to learn about the world, experience life directly, and build her self-confidence and abilities, we encourage the development of an inner moral sense and responsibility. *It is far more effective to be positive with young children rather than negative.* The more a child is able to pursue his natural course of development, the happier and more self-disciplined he will be.

Provide learning materials

Disposable plastic toys are like sugary treats for your child's brain. They provide a jolt of fun and excitement, followed by a quick crash. Good learning materials provide real food for brain development. Children understand this intuitively and are powerfully drawn to them. This book will show you how to create your own learning materials and give you examples of good ones to buy. Diverting a portion of your toy budget for birthdays and holidays to buying learning materials will be a wonderful investment in your child's brain development and future.

Introduce math & reading

Read with your child every day. Let her pick out books she is really interested in, and talk about them before, during, and after you read. Look for opportunities to introduce counting up to 10 identical objects carefully. Do this before you introduce your child to written numerals, as these are more abstract than actual objects. When your child shows interest in numbers and letters, start the **Math** (p. 131) and **Reading** (p. 152) sequences. The activities in these chapters follow each other in a logical way to help your child develop these skills efficiently.

Encourage socialization

Young children need to learn that they live in a world full of other people and must learn to get along with them. Manners and common courtesy should be taught consistently to every young child.

Parents doing early learning at home should always be on the lookout for ways to get their children together with other children for play dates and work with early learning materials. As long as your child is okay with it, invite another child or two over, show them how to use the materials, and let all of them freely work and play as they see fit. Let them find their own way as much as possible. Intervene only to suggest better ways of resolving differences and stop any inappropriate behavior. If they each want to do something on their own, fine. If they want to work together on something, that's fine also. Let the children play and work. Once freed from the expectation of seeking the approval of adults for everything they do, kids change.

Organized play groups, the playground, children's concerts and events - all can be opportunities for socialization experiences. If you can find enough willing parents and children, a *preschool coop* is a wonderful idea.

Provide excellent nutrition

The daily food guide recommends the following for young children:

- **4 to 5 daily servings of fruits and vegetables**
- **3 to 4 daily servings of grains**
- **2 servings of milk and milk alternatives**
- **1 serving of meat and alternatives**

Too much refined sugar, fatty meats, and highly processed, empty calorie foods, especially fast foods, negatively impact a child's physical and mental development. Search the internet for the many posts on preparing healthy foods that children will eat. With some flexibility, creativity, and imagination, even picky eaters can receive excellent nutrition.

See the Practical Life section (p.56) for ideas on involving your child in kitchen activities. One of the best ways to get a preschooler interested in good food and nutrition is to get him helping with fun food projects in the kitchen. Cooks love to taste their work!

Using Early Learning Materials At Home

Young children have a deep inner need to **explore the world through all their senses and hold and manipulate objects with their hands**. The typical toys of early childhood often do not meet these developmental needs. Disposable plastic toys are like sugary treats for your child's brain. They provide a rush of excitement that fades, leaving the child looking for the next new toy. This helps toy companies thrive, not children.

The learning materials found in Montessori and other quality preschools, in contrast, provide real food for brain development. They have none of the whiz-bang features of the toys that line the shelves at the store, yet children have found them fascinating for over one hundred years. This is because they meet young children's powerful inner need to learn, adapt, and grow.

Well-designed learning materials teach children simply by being handled. As children explore and manipulate these objects, they absorb all kinds of sensory impressions and make discoveries through movement and free exploration. This is the essence of early learning for 2-6 year olds. Home learning materials should be a mix of those you make yourself, plus a selection of Montessori and other good commercial materials. You will find these listed on pages 40 - 42. You do not have to get all of these, but a nice selection will complement the materials you will see on the coming pages.

Home early learning need not be expensive. If you divert just half the money you would otherwise spend on plastic disposable toys at Christmas and on birthdays over 2-3 years to buying learning materials, your budget will not even notice it. Working with a child for 2 years, you can buy all the materials needed to make most of the activities shown in this book for about the cost of a Starbuck's latte and a muffin a week.

This book will show you how to make wonderful materials using common items that are available almost anywhere. I made and used all these materials in three different Montessori preschools over more than a decade, and found that they work beautifully. The directions for each activity will tell you what you need and how to put things together. Here is a list of some of the items you will need:

bowls	unpopped popcorn	colored wood beads	child safe scissors
muffin tin	grape nuts cereal	colored paper clips	funnels
cookie sheet	uncooked rice	colored rubber bands	various jars w/ lids
measuring cups	salt	coins, all kinds	cheese slicer
measuring spoons	sugar	colored string & yarn	plastic knives
coffee cups	pasta, diff shapes	construction paper	golf tees
plain glass cups	beans, diff kinds	card stock, colored	marbles
paper/foam cups	egg cartons	white glue	ruler
plastic food boxes	food boxes	glue stick	single hole punch
plastic bucket	dry coffee	computer, printer	stapler
small baskets	ice cube tray	spices	buttons, all kinds
small trays	baster	spice grinder	shoelaces
serving spoons	kitchen tongs	small gravy ladle	small hand mirror
sponges	eyedroppers	straws	tweezers
small cloths	whisk	self-stick labels	condiment cups
food coloring	OJ hand juicer	clothespins	foam pom poms
foam flower blocks	sm cutting board	play doh set	sm dustpan set
diff fabrics	coin wrappers	blindfold	cotton balls
magnet	comb	magnifying glass	paper

Making self-contained materials

Below are two home made early learning materials. Each one is self-contained on its own tray. You can also use bowls, small boxes, baskets, even plates, to hold learning materials. This makes them easy to display on low shelves for easy access. Common objects look different and special on their own tray. They hold the promise of new, fun things to do. Your child can get them from the shelf, use them, and put them back, all by herself. This helps a child **focus concentration**, which is the key to developing brain architecture, self-discipline, and a love of learning.

Button Sorting by color   **Spooning Corn**

These materials each **isolate** a specific activity. They use common items in new and interesting ways. The tray on the left is a material for sorting buttons by color. It is organized and attractive. The colors of paper circles in the containers match the colors of the buttons. The buttons are all the same size. This isolates color as the determining factor in how the buttons are sorted. If the buttons were different shapes and sizes, the purpose of the activity would not be as clear. There are the same number of each color of button – 3 in this case. Activities like this are appropriate for 2-3 year olds, and provide opportunities to introduce new language and counting.

The material on the right on the previous page is a **Transfer** activity (p. 59). These activities involve moving something back and forth between containers using various tools. This material uses wood, ceramic, metal, and food elements to create an aesthetic looking material with many points of interest. The color of the corn stands out in the white bowls. The spoon is grasped in a certain way. The corn makes an interesting sound as it falls into the empty bowl. All these little points of interest help focus a child's attention. The tray has a lip to catch most kernels of corn that are spilled so the child can more easily pick them up. Good homemade learning materials:

- **Are self-contained on a tray or in a box, bowl, or basket**
- **Are organized, attractive, and have points of interest**
- **Isolate the skill or feature of the activity; and**
- **Include a Control of Error**

The Control of Error in the button sorting material is seeing buttons of different colors in the same container. When a child is ready to see this it will be obvious, and that will guide the child to making corrections. Seeing corn outside the bowls is the control of error in the transfer material. Children should be encouraged to **pick up any spills as soon as they occur**, as this is all part of the activity.

Create self-contained materials for as many of the activities in this book as possible. Place commercial materials in nice boxes and bowls. These can all go on your child's shelves for easy access.

Demonstrating materials for your child

When you show your child a new material, it helps to give a brief, careful demonstration of how to use the material before you turn it over to your child. This may seem odd, but this is how it is done in Montessori schools, and it really helps a child focus attention on the activity. By your careful handling and use of the material, you communicate that it is a special item worthy of respect.

When demonstrating materials, move slowly and carefully. Handle the objects very carefully, slowly exaggerating your movements so your child can clearly see. Speak very little, if at all, perhaps just saying a few words to show the points of interest. With transfer activities, always spill a little material and then immediately stop and pick up or clean up the spill. This helps your child remember to do the same. Your movements become a 'template' for your child.

The Activity Cycle

The Activity Cycle is another helpful technique for encouraging children to focus their attention and develop an organized approach to their work. When a child wants to use a material, he:

1. **Sets out a small floor rug or table mat to make a 'work area';**
2. **Brings the material to this work area and uses it;**
3. **Cleans up and puts the material away; and**
4. **Puts the rug or mat away.**

This may seem a bit formal to parents working with their children at home, but it teaches children excellent habits. They learn to prepare before doing something, to approach tasks in an organized way, and to finish what they start. You may or may not find that using the Activity Cycle works at your house, but I encourage you to give it a try. It elevates children's work to a level deserving of respect, and helps children focus attention – the key to early learning.

Displaying learning materials

Early learning materials should never be thrown in a toy box or catch-all toy drawer. You want to emphasize that these materials are special and deserve respect. The best way to demonstrate this, and make materials very accessible for your child to choose and use independently, is to **display them on low shelves in an attractive way**. Here are some examples:

familygosimple.com

Left: chasingcheerios.blogspot.com
Right: jen-peacefulparenting.blogspot.com

chasingcheerios.blogspot.com

These displays highlight each material as a special item and help a child internalize a sense of beauty and order. It is necessary to organize and keep the materials ready for use each day. This does not take long, and will make your child's home early learning much more effective.

The materials that are out on the shelves should be those your child is most interested in using at that time. You will see your child's interest's change as new materials are made available and she gets older. The materials should change along with her interests.

> *"Besides the various objects which the children are taught to use for their 'practical life', there are many others which lend themselves to the gradual development and refinement of a child's intellect. There are various materials for the education of the senses, for learning the alphabet, numbers, reading, writing, and arithmetic.....When we speak of 'environment' we include the sum total of objects which a child can freely choose and use as he pleases, according to his needs and tendencies. A teacher simply assists him at the beginning to get his bearings among so many different things and teaches him the precise use of each of them....she introduces him to the ordered and active life of the environment."*

Maria Montessori, *The Discovery of the Child*

When a parent acts as a child's teacher, she does the same thing - **create an environment rich in opportunities for meaningful, interesting activity and introduce the child to the materials it contains**. She helps sparingly, and introduces new materials when the child is ready and interested, always following the child and the Inner Teacher.

Finding the right materials for your child

Follow your child's interests. Trust the Inner Teacher, present a variety of materials, and let your child choose what she is interested in every day. Watch for any new spark of interest in colors, numbers, shapes, words, science activities, or anything else; and make materials and provide experiences that allow a child to explore that area more. It's a dynamic, fluid process.

Portioning nuts at Tot School

Follow the child is the guiding principle of Montessori. But where do you start with *your* child? I'll give you a few suggestions for different ages. The **Ages & Activities Chart** on page 34 shows a progression of activities. Use these ideas to help you get started. Another way is to look through the activity photos with your child and let her choose which ones she'd like to do. You will not have a complete preschool in your home with all the activities out all the time. You will need to experiment, try different activities, and use your child's interest as your guide. This will be an ongoing process. Not every material you make will be a hit, and that's okay. The materials your child loves will make up for it.

Start with a **Practical Life** (p. 56) or **Sensorial** (p. 76) material. These materials are the foundation of early learning for 2 ½ - 6 year old children. They set the stage for the science, math, and language activities that follow. These activities and materials:

- Open millions of brain nerve pathways and build strong brain architecture

- Give children a series of successes that build a confident self-image

- Help children learn to focus their concentration

- Support and encourage a young child's strong drive toward independence

- Refine and educate a child's senses

- Develop muscle control and coordination

- Develop abstract thinking skills and prepare the child for reading and mathematics

- Help children become participants in life instead of spectators

Here are good starter Practical Life and Sensorial materials:

2 ½ - 3 ½ years

Rice Tub, p. 58	Rice Pouring, p. 59	Play Doh. p. 61
Pasta Sorting, p. 77	Pink Tower, p. 82	Bead Threading p. 66

3 – 4 years

Shapes Lacing, p. 66	Binomial Cube, p. 86	Tongs & Balls, p. 59
Keys & Locks, p. 71	Water Transfer, p. 60	Sorting Coins, p. 77

When starting with a 4-6 year old child, let her choose any of the Practical Life or Sensorial activities that interest her. See the next heading about the Learning Sweet Spot to help you see if a material is too easy, too difficult, or just about right. Around 4, many children enter a natural sensitive period for learning about written language and mathematics. Observe your child for this and, when the interest is there, start the math and reading activities.

The Learning Sweet Spot

An activity in the Learning Sweet Spot **holds your child's interest and attention, and she will want to repeat it, even if she makes mistakes**. These are always the activities you are looking for. Activities that are too easy cause **boredom** and a lack of interest. Activities that are too difficult cause **frustration**. These are extremes to avoid, particularly frustration. A frustrated child may be turned off to learning activities for a while. Here is a graphic depiction of the Learning Sweet Spot:

Boredom   **Sweet Spot**   **Frustration**

The Learning Sweet Spot is just a bit toward the frustration end. The activity will challenge your child and he will not master it right away, but that will not stop him from wanting to continue until he does master it, which would likely happen if he became frustrated.

The key is to find materials that excite your child's interest and focus his attention, and that he repeats using. When your child masters a material or skill, provide something a bit more challenging.

Repetition is a vital part of early learning. When a child repeats using a favorite material, brain nerve networks are created and strengthened. Repetition is essential for skills mastery and brain development. Allow your child **uninterrupted time** to work with favorite materials.

Sequencing

Many skills are developed by mastering a series of progressively more difficult component skills. The **Transfer** activities (p. 59) are a good example. Starting with a whole hand grasp, a child moves gradually to a writing grasp over time. **Math and reading** are more examples of sequentially developed skills. Follow the activities in the sequences shown and give your child plenty of practice and repetition at each step.

The chart on the next page can help you find appropriate activities.

Ages & Activities

These are only suggestions. **Your child may be ready earlier or later than the ages shown.** Use your child's enthusiasm level and abilities as your guides. *Follow the child.*

Age	Practical Life	Sensorial	Language	Math
3	Rice tub Transfers with water, plain cups, rice Threading beads Cleaning a table Fabric folding	Play Doh Knobbed cylinders Knobless cylinders Pink Tower Red Rods	Reading to your child daily (continues as long as possible)	Sorting Threading beads Transfers Pink Tower Red Rods Shape Sets & Groups
4	Banana cutting Lacing Transfers with handles, lips, tongs, tweezers Pipe building Nuts & Bolts Clothing fasteners	Rough/smooth Sorting Color Cards Color Mixing Geo Board Mystery Bag Binomial Cube Fabric Matching Touch Matching Color Shades Geometric Solids Circles & Squares grading Sound Matching	Sandpaper Letters Letter writing Phonetic Word building	Geometric Shapes Sandpaper Numerals Amounts & Numerals 0-100
5	Cutting celery Helping clean the house Make a shopping list Use simple tools Painting a wall	Trinomial Cube Smell & Taste matching	Phonetic Reading Sight Words Reading	Addition, Subtraction, Multiplication, Fractions Decimal system Practical uses of numbers
6				

The Three Step Lesson

We teach our children many names for things. The Three Step Lesson helps children move names from **short term memory** into **long term memory**. Young children are building their brain 'memory banks', so using a technique that assists them in this process makes sense. Maria Montessori developed this tool just for this purpose. Here is how it works, in this case to teach a child the color names **yellow**, **red**, and **blue**. The materials are paint sample cards from the hardware store, one each in yellow, red, and blue. It works the same with almost any object, letter, numeral, amount, etc.

1. Identify

Show the child each paint card, *one at a time*, hiding the other two. Say the name of the color. Hand the card to your child and have her say the name of the color as she looks at the card. You can look for objects in your house that are the same color. Do this with each of the three color cards.

2. Recognize

Set out *all three* cards. Ask, *"Can you point to the blue one?"* Repeat with the other two colors. Have your child close his eyes while you change the positions of the cards. Repeat, asking your child to point out each color. Place the cards on a table across the room and ask your child to go and bring back each color in turn. Switch roles and have your child ask you to point out the colors. Play many games like this. This step is when the names move from short term into long term memory.

3. Remember

Show your child each card again, *one at a time*, hiding the other two. Ask your child *"What color is this?"* Repeat with each card.

If your child does not remember one or more color names in step three, start over again in step one and repeat the process. Sometimes it takes a few repetitions. You can make it easier by using two instead of three objects, and by only doing steps one and two a couple of times before you do step three. Always keep things positive and do something else if you notice any frustration developing in your child. Pressure and stress are to be avoided.

Use three step lessons to teach your child all the colors, geometric shapes, types of materials (glass, metal, plastic, fabric, etc.), amounts and numerals in math, phonetic sounds and sight words in reading, types of fruit and vegetables, the names of tools, types of furniture, all kinds of things. **Anytime you are teaching your child the name for something, you can use a Three Step Lesson.**

Record Keeping

Most preschools keep a record of what materials and activities each child is using. This reminds Teachers where a child is at, especially when they begin the math and reading sequences. We know what the child did the last time and can see when he has mastered something and may be ready to move to something a bit more challenging. At home, this can be done very simply by writing down the date your child works with a material, and whether it was:

I – introduced that day for the first time;

P – your child practiced with it; or

M – your child has mastered the material or skill.

Taking the time to write this down will help you keep up on where your child is at with materials in different areas.

Safety

Maintaining safety is your first priority. In a Montessori preschool, children freely choose their activities. They are carefully monitored; and not allowed to work carelessly or create dangerous situations. This is also essential in the home.

Choking and ingestion hazards

Many materials use small objects which a child can swallow and cause choking. If your child explores the world orally, hold off on these activities until she is a bit older. Every parent should take a **Basic Life Support (BLS) course**. Know how to **clear an airway**.

Sharp points and edges

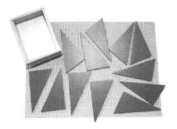

Montessori materials, in particular, are precisely made and have sharper edges and corner points than typical plastic toys. Do not allow your child to handle them carelessly or throw them about.

Montessori Constructive Triangles

Chemical hazards

There are many good toxin-free cleaning products your child can use in Practical Life activities and around your home. Switching to these types of products is good for everyone. Make learning to use a spray bottle an activity in itself. Be sure your child can safely use one before he tries spraying cleaning solution.

Electrical hazards

About 2400 children are electrocuted every year. There are many good options for child-proofing electrical outlets. Traditional outlet hole caps can be removed pretty easily; and you may forget to replace them after you use an outlet. Take a look at the various types of covers that work better. Remember to safety-proof surge protector outlets, also.

Burn hazards

Adjust your water heater so your child cannot scald his skin. 120 degrees F is the generally recommended safe maximum for hot water in a home. Obviously, if a science experiment uses heat, such as a candle, extra care is required.

Independence has risks and responsibilities. Give your child time to practice skills **under close supervision**. Always keep a watchful eye on her activities. **Allow him to use materials independently only when he has shown the clear ability to do so safely**.

'Safety First'

Using printable materials

Printed materials can be handled and arranged in ways that digital images cannot. They allow children to hold, examine, and absorb an image before it zooms away. Parents can download and print the same high quality printables used in Montessori schools. A few of the many good sources for printables are listed below. Get familiar with what these sites have to offer, and also check out their free printables.

Montessori Print Shop

Montessori For Everyone

Enchanted Learning

1+1+1=1

First School

Education.com

Kidsparkz.com

To use downloaded printables, you will need a color computer printer, 67 & 110 lb. card stock in white and colors, scissors, glue sticks, stapler, ruler, single hole punch, colorful yarn, and perhaps some no-heat laminating sheets. You will find directions for creating your printables on the Montessori Print Shop site.

Montessori Three Part Cards

Also called **Nomenclature Cards,** these are graphic tools Montessori created to help children learn with images and words. They are excellent for home use, and all kinds of cards are available.

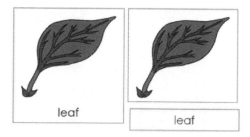

The three parts are a card with an image, a card with a word, and a card with both the image and the word.

A description of how to use Three Part Cards can be found online at Montessori Print Shop. Here are typical presentations for different ages:

The **picture cards without labels** are used with **2-3 year olds** to enrich their language. Show them a picture and, using clear speech, say the name of the picture. Ask them to repeat the word.

The **picture cards with labels** are used for **3-4 year olds who are getting into words**. You can use these cards to play games like "I Spy". This helps children to make connections between letters and sounds. For instance, using pictures of woodland animals - "*I spy with my little eye an animal that starts with the sound 'buh' ..... can you show me an animal that starts with the sound 'buh'?*" (bear).

The **picture cards without the labels and the labels** are used for children who are reading, usually **4-5 years** of age. The point now is to read the labels and match them to the objects that they are already familiar with - it's a reading lesson. They read the labels, match them to the pictures, and use the labeled picture cards to check their work.

Children can also simply explore with the cards, arranging them as they desire. There are many more wonderful printables that will add greatly to your home early learning. Other examples and sources are found throughout the book with specific activities.

Montessori materials for home use

The prices of original Montessori classroom materials have come down over the years. Pictured here is a suggested selection for home use. These will be a wonderful addition to your home preschool. These materials are available online at sites such as:

Montessori Outlet	**Kid Advance Montessori**
Adena Montessori	**A plus Montessori**

If kept in decent condition, Montessori materials can be sold for up to half their original cost when your child is finished with them.

Knobbed Cylinder Block #1 has 10 cylinders that increase in height and decrease in diameter. Great for 2-3 yr. olds.

The **#3 Cylinder Block** cylinders decrease in height and increase in diameter. This and the #1 block are fine for home use.

The **Knobless Cylinders** have all the cylinders of the four Cylinder Blocks, color coded and with each set in its own beautiful box. Great for free building exploration and matching to control cards.

The **Red Rods** go from 10 cm to 1 meter in length. These are big for home use, instructions are given for making your own mini-set.

The **Pink Tower** is possibly the most recognized Montessori material. Children 2-4 love it. Pairing the Tower with the Brown Stair creates all kinds of building possibilities.

The versatile **Blue Constructive Triangles** are only around $11, and allow your child to make all kinds of plane shapes and figures.

The **Brown Stair** (also called the Broad Stair), is a bit expensive but, paired with a Pink Tower, offers myriad building opportunities.

Every preschooler should have a **Mystery Bag with Geometric Shapes**. This inexpensive material has a couple of nice drawstring bags and a great double set of cool wooden geometric solid shapes.

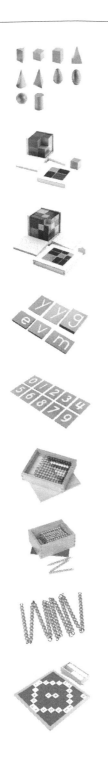

The **Geometric Solids** are pricey, but they are beautiful and children absorb all kinds of information just by handling them.

The **Binomial Cube** displays the Binomial Theorem in three dimensions. For kids, it's a cool box with blocks that fit like a puzzle.

When your child masters the Binomial Cube, the **Trinomial Cube** will extend the challenge.

The block style, lower case **Sandpaper Letters** are a must when your child begins the Reading Sequence. Try making your own and risk losing your sanity!

The block style **Sandpaper Numerals** are used when starting the Math Sequence.

The **Teen Bead Bar Box** is inexpensive and used for many activities in the Math Sequence.

A box of **45 Golden Bead Ten Bars** is handy to have when your child starts working with larger quantities up to 100.

The **Hundred Golden Bead Chain** costs less than $5 and is used in many math activities. A real bargain!

The **Hundred Board** is a beautiful, classic math material that is used for many math activities and to illustrate math concepts.

More good early learning materials

More high quality early learning materials are available from a number of good suppliers, including these:

Melissa & Doug **Edushape** **Guidecraft** **Montessori Services**

Learning Resources **Lakeshore** **Brio** **Growing Tree Toys**

Examples of quality early learning materials found online at the suppliers above include:

Geometric Stackers	Guidecraft Texture Dominoes
Inchimals	Colorful Caterpillars Game
Melissa & Doug Pattern Blocks	Classic Wooden Abacus
Edushape Tricky Fingers	Potholder Loom Set
Mindware Pattern Play	Wooden Pound-a-Peg
Life on Earth Memory Matching	Drillin' Action Tool Set
Wooden Shape Sorting Clock	Melissa & Doug Magnetic Calendar
Leapfrog Scribble & Write	Lauri Toys Shapes & Colors Sorter
Channel Craft Toy Tin Marbles	Whammo Soft Catch Frisbee
Brio Ultimate Building Set	Lego Ultimate Building Set
Tommy Gearation Gear Magnets	Richard Scarry Busytown
Gears, Gears, Gears	Alex Toys String a Farm
12" Inflatable Globe	Pretend & Play Cash register
Bug viewers	Magnifying glasses
Microscopes	Telescopes

These are just a few ideas. Search online for the best prices. A selection of these and some of the Montessori materials make wonderful additions to your child's home preschool. They will look great on her shelves along with materials you make. Your child will get more brain-building experiences from these materials than from all the disposable plastic toys you could buy. Early learning materials are a wonderful investment in your child's future.

Summary

Make it fun. Early learning should be fun experiences and discoveries.

Follow your child. Let your child's interests be your guide. Observe your child, see what she is interested in, and do activities around that. Suggest things to do and bring out new things when your child is open but has not chosen anything to do that day.

Mix homemade and commercial materials. A nice mix gives your child many options for focusing her attention. Use Montessori principles when making your materials. Substitute good learning materials for disposable plastic toys.

Display materials rather than use a toy box. Early learning is almost impossible if your child has to rummage around in a toy box. Help your child tidy up her shelves and materials to be ready for use each day.

Encourage the Activity Cycle. Creating work spaces and finishing activities by putting them away has numerous benefits.

Aim for the Learning Sweet Spot. An activity that is just challenging enough to take some practice to master; and that your child eagerly uses until she masters it, is in her Learning Sweet Spot. Boredom and frustration are the extremes to avoid.

Demonstrate new activities and materials. Your demonstration shows your child how to handle materials carefully, with respect. You can show points of interest and how to clean up spills. Demonstrations show that you respect the materials and your child should, also.

Encourage independent work and repetition. You should not be leading your child's activities most of the time. Cooperative work like cooking and reading together is great; but your child also needs to develop a self-directed, self-motivated approach to his activities. Repetition is essential for skills mastery and brain development.

Help your child follow a gradual path to abstract thought. Always start with hands-on materials. Introduce printed materials and tablet and computer experiences when your child is ready. Include printed words and numerals as appropriate.

FAQ's

I have a toddler and a preschooler. How can I keep the younger child from disrupting the older child's work?

Many parents deal with this. Here are some ideas from them:

- Work with the toddler to teach her that she is not allowed to touch the older child's work. With most toddlers, this will involve anger and frustration at first. You should be calmly consistent in not allowing the toddler to touch or disrupt the older child's work. He will accept it eventually. This will be good practice for similar situations later!

- If the children have separate rooms, great. The older child's things can be displayed and primarily used, in his room. This solves most of the issues; but is not possible for many parents.

- Encourage your older child to use her materials when the younger child naps.

- Display the older child's materials out of reach of the younger child. This is important, as the younger child will not be ready to care for materials properly and will create disorganization. This will prevent the older child from seeing her materials as special.

- Always provide something for the younger child to do when the older child is using a material. Your toddler can have his own shelves and baskets for materials appropriate for her age, which will help him become familiar with this way of displaying materials and putting them back.

- Do cooperative projects. Art projects and cooking in the kitchen are two classic areas for this. Choose a cooking project that both children can contribute to. Find things the toddler can do - mixing by hand in a bowl, scooping out food, handing you plates - while the older child is doing things requiring more skill and motor control. Congratulate and thank both children when the project is done. Your daily reading time is another good option for cooperative activity.

- When the toddler is ready to use one of the older child's early materials, have the older child show him how. Children often learn best from other children.

We don't have enough space to have a lot of materials out at one time. What can we do?

Do the best you can, few situations are ideal. Try to find a place for one small set of shelves to display the activities your child is most keen on at any given time. Look for other places you may not have considered to display materials, such as the top of a dresser, a drawer in a chest or nightstand, a cabinet, or a table top. Stacked plastic storage drawers on wheels in a closet can hold quite a few materials. One Mom uses the new jug style plastic coffee containers and puts a material, or a couple of materials, in each, with a photo of the activity glued to the outside. She stacks and lines these up, making great use of a small space. Use drawers under the bed for clothes, and a couple of dresser drawers for materials. If you get creative, you'll find a way. Even if you have to store materials in a closet and get them out when you can, your child will still benefit.

My child does not treat the learning materials we make and those I have purchased with respect. He throws them and knocks them around, then goes back to his other toys. What can I do?

The activities shown here are learning experiences, not toys. If these types of materials are new to your child, and your child is used to treating toys roughly, transitioning to learning materials can take a while.

Be patient. Demonstrate each material so your child gets an idea that this is a special activity. Display materials differently than your child's toys, on their own shelves. You will need to remove materials that your child handles roughly and abuses. Tell him he can use them when he is able to take care of them. You might have to take all your child's toys away until he shows the ability to take care of them. That may seem extreme, but it can be required with some children.

Teachers in Montessori schools have it a bit easier than parents. They don't have the interpersonal relationship a parent builds up with their child. They are starting fresh with new rules in a new environment. There is also the peer aspect. They see other children working and tend to realize and accept that this is how it's done here. Parents who observe the class in session are often amazed that that is their child out there!

The result you are working towards is a moment **when your child's attention is captured by a material and he repeats using it with focused concentration**. That is the real goal. The more focused concentration you see, the more your child will develop self-discipline and an inner focus that will positively impact her outer behavior. Keep trying materials until you see spontaneous, focused attention. That is when you have hit the mark. The rest will follow. Rotate new materials onto the shelves when your child has mastered the current materials or shows little interest in them anymore.

In some home situations, it may be best to bring out materials slowly, one at a time, so your child can focus on using each one. Putting too many new materials out too quickly can backfire. It is usually best to start slowly and demonstrate no more than one new material every few days or every week in a home setting.

"An interesting piece of work, freely chosen, which has the virtue of inducing concentration rather than fatigue, adds to the child's energies and mental capacities, and leads him to self-mastery."

Maria Montessori

My child is hyperactive and won't sit still for me to demonstrate materials. He grabs at them and gets angry when he cannot do it right away. What can I do?

This happens to many parents. Teachers usually have an easier time because the children don't know them yet so they often tread more lightly! Even teachers face this issue, though. You may find that using materials that immediately allow a child to get busy with them work better to start. Legos, sorting materials, a sensory bin, and hammering are examples. You can also team up for activities like washing a table or cooking. Working along with you sometimes helps a child slow down and pay attention to what is happening.

Hyperactive children today are the same children who played for hours outside many years ago. In our TV, internet, and scary neighborhoods world, we can forget how much large muscle movement young children need. Provide more opportunities for your child to play and move outside. Hyperactivity is not necessarily a problem or the beginning of ADHD. Your child probably just needs more large muscle movement free play before he will calm down enough to concentrate on learning materials. If you keep trying and are patient, you will eventually find materials your child is drawn to concentrate on – that is your goal. Once this starts happening regularly, your child will gain more self-control.

Don't these activities require trained teachers? What if I mess something up?

This is preschool we're talking here, you can handle it! As long as your heart is in the right place and you stay patient, positive, and encourage your child's efforts, you will be fine. The world won't end if an activity does not go as planned. Make something positive out of it and move on. If today does not bring a big success, tomorrow will, relax and enjoy your child. Most of these activities are pretty fail safe. Many are designed to allow a child to pursue them independently. All experiences are food for brain development in early childhood. Follow your child's lead and the activity descriptions. Have fun!

I just want to teach my child math and reading. Is the other stuff really important?

Yes. The Practical Life and Sensorial activities are the all-important foundation of early learning for 2-6 year old children. They set the stage for math and reading. They develop visual acuity and discrimination, left-to-right visual patterning, the ability to concentrate, small muscle control and coordination, strong brain architecture, the ability to use abstract thought, and a positive self-image. Children who do these activities regularly find learning math, reading, and everything else that comes later much easier.

If your child is around 2-3 when you start doing activities that is perfect. You can do Practical Life and Sensorial activities until he shows signs of entering his sensitive period for math and reading. If your child is 4-6 when you start doing activities, let him explore the Practical Life and Sensorial activities at the same time you try the math and reading activities. Children have a built-in tendency to fill in gaps in their own development. She may not do the earlier activities for as long as a younger child; but they will still be very valuable.

What signs should I look for to tell me my child's learning activities are having a positive impact on her development?

Early learning activities help children learn to **concentrate**, which helps them be calmer and better able to focus on tasks. A more even disposition, the ability to focus attention for significant periods of time, and positive demonstrations of independence are some of the benefits of early learning activities. This takes time.

The goals of early learning are to create strong brain architecture, not to be reading novels or doing algebra by 5. The ultimate value of early learning is not always evident until a child grows up into a person who excels in school, can multi-task, loves learning new things, has self-confidence, and can get along with others. These are the true benefits. Early learning is an all-important investment in your child's future.

As your child does more **Practical Life** activities, you should see her ability to control objects with her hands increase. She should, by using progressively more challenging tools, be working ultimately toward using a proper writing grasp. This takes time and practice, so resist the urge or expectation for her to master this quickly. He should also become able to pour his own drinks without spilling, and know how to clean up if he does. She should start getting her own snacks, and learn to dress herself. Practical Life skills are an area where you see pretty definite results in a child's development, as long as he has the chance to work with them regularly. You should see your child gradually become more independent and confident.

The **Sensorial** materials likewise promote focused concentration. Your child should start to be able to differentiate colors, sizes, and shapes. When you get started with the **Math and Reading Sequences**, you will be able to follow your child's progress more easily and clearly.

My child is only three and she already knows her numbers up to twenty and her alphabet. Why does she need to learn more than that?

Parents may think that if their child memorizes and can verbally repeat the sequence of numbers and the letters of the alphabet, he has achieved an understanding of numbers and language. Actually, these are simply exercises in memorization. The child could just as well have memorized a sequence of color names, a song, or the parts of a car. It's all just words; the child usually has little or no true understanding yet.

Early learning materials give a child a hands-on, deep understanding of each area. Math work starts with identifying groups of actual objects. It then progresses through learning numerals, and then matching the amounts to the numerals. Reading begins with one sound for each letter; and progresses through simple word building and on into sight words, sentences, and actual reading. In each case, real understanding is achieved by progressing through a logical sequence of activities that teach **real skills through practice over a significant period of time.**

In first grade, a child who has simply memorized numeral and letter sequences will be almost as bewildered by actual math and reading work as a child who knows nothing of math and reading. A child who has progressed even partly through the math and reading sequences shown here, however, will have a firm foundation of actual skills to build on. Memorization does not equal understanding.

How can I put together an organized plan for my child's early learning? Where do I find preschool lesson plans?

Many parents want to plan out their child's activities. Structure makes us feel like we're in control and not leaving anything out. Most of us attended structured schools using lesson plans and fixed curricula, so that is what we equate with 'real' education. Many traditional preschools work from lesson plans and weekly activity guides and offer wonderful experiences. Early learning actually works best, however, with a different approach, called trusting the Inner Teacher and **following the child**.

Young children are in a unique period of development, guided by an Inner Teacher. They have an **inner motivation, curiosity, and drive** to reach out to understand and experience life. There is an intelligent design at work guiding their development. Young children are not aimless, empty vessels dependent on us to fill them up with knowledge. They are already fully equipped to absorb their environment and learn how to function in it. Whether adults help children much or not, children learn to walk, talk, think, control their bodies, and begin learning at least the rudiments of math and language in their early years. They are programmed by nature to accomplish this great feat of development.

If we trust the Inner Teacher and **create a rich environment of activities, materials, and experiences**, young children will spontaneously reach out to explore it. It is through those **self-initiated explorations** that they learn the best. They also learn to trust their own instincts and interests, and become **independent, self-guided learners**. This provides the best possible preparation for school and life beyond. It also means that most children pick things up a bit faster than expected! This is why children in Montessori schools learn math and reading at early ages.

What Maria Montessori asked was, *"Can we **help life** as it naturally unfolds in the child?"* She didn't assume we had to direct the process. Instead, she created a **beautiful, rich environment** where each child could achieve more of their potential via their own efforts, choices, work, and achievements. She gave them the freedom, space, and tools to develop in an optimal way. **The child provides the motivation**. Rather than create children who learn to be dependent on adults to tell them what comes next, a properly prepared environment teaches children to trust themselves, act on their own initiative, and experience their own learning rewards. When you give children this opportunity, their development takes off. That is one reason children in Montessori schools learn math, reading, and science so much earlier than is 'typical' for young children. Their natural development is given freedom, encouragement, and help in the form of well-designed environment full of cool learning materials, and marvelous things happen.

The role of a Montessori teacher, and of parents using these ideas at home, is that of a **guide and mentor**. You help your child **create materials, keep the environment ready** for use, and **demonstrate** new materials. You **observe** your child to see if materials are too difficult, too easy, or offer just about the right degree of challenge. When your child masters information or a skill, you **provide something a bit more challenging**.

If you follow the information here and create hands-on materials displayed on low shelves, your child will eventually respond and begin using them. One important way to encourage this is to **strictly limit TV and tablet screen time.** Video screens are incredibly seductive to children of all ages. Too much exposure to them in the early years can short circuit a child's development. **Young children need to move their bodies, engage all their senses in real world activities, and directly relate to other people**. If you provide learning materials and limit screen time, your child will naturally find her way into using them. This will open up a whole new experience for both you and your child as he masters real skills and builds strong brain architecture. The result will be a more confident, competent child well prepared for life, rather than a zombie addicted to video screens.

You can be a great home teaching parent!

One of the beautiful things about many of the activities is that even very young children can use them **independently**. Children open up millions of new brain nerve circuits simply by handling and using these activities. With many activities, you role is as a **facilitator** and **helper.** You help create and maintain your child's home environment. You demonstrate materials and then then turn them over to your child to use as long as she wants. Most often **the material is the teacher**, not you.

Some of the activities require your direct participation. You will show your child how to do all kinds of Practical Life activities. Matching up sounds, weights, fabrics, and smells while your child wears a blindfold requires your involvement. Teaching your child the names of objects, colors, amounts, numbers, letters, etc., can be done using **Three Step Lessons** (p. 35). You will help your child as he starts reading his first books. There will be plenty for you to do.

Part of the art of helping a young child is in knowing when to actively help and when to step back. Learning should be a process of discovery. Your child needs room to make mistakes and encouragement to keep trying. Too much of your help and your child will give up and let you do it. Too little, and your child may feel you don't care about what he is doing. You'll have to find the balance on your own. That's part of the growing process for you as a parent. Children teach us, too. Help only as needed and then let your child explore activities.

One of your big roles will be to **closely observe** your own child. What activities does he like to do the most? Which ones does he repeat? What kinds of things is he interested in today, this week, this month? Is he getting frustrated or bored, or is an activity just about right for his skill level? Which activities might be good for him to do next? The best advice I can offer is to:

Be patient, be positive, and
encourage your child's efforts.

Be patient. Slow down and explore the *process* of doing these activities. With early learning, the journey is the destination. These activities should be fun, happy experiences. Give your child plenty of time and space to explore, create, discover, and make mistakes. It's all part of the brain building process. Stress or pressure may turn your child off to learning activities altogether. **Early learning is not a competition or a race. Children develop according to an inner timetable, so go with the flow**. If your child needs help to learn something, provide it in a positive way. Never rush a child to learn. Follow your child's lead and you won't go wrong. This should be a fun process. Avoid comparing your child's progress with other children.

Be positive. Create a **positive verbal environment**. Talk with your child about what he is doing. Encourage him to express his thoughts, and then listen. Ask a variety of questions like, *"Tell me more about that"*, *"What happened then?"*, or *"And then what?"* Look at your child when she is talking and nod your head or otherwise indicate that you are listening. This shows the child that you respect and appreciate her activities and what she has to say.

Make **reflective** and **encouraging** statements. A reflective statement summarizes, without judgment, what your child is doing. Examples would be, *"You are cutting the banana,"* *"You are sorting the beads by color,"* and *"You are cleaning the table."* An encouraging statement does just that – it offers encouragement. Examples: *"Don't worry, everyone spills sometimes, keep trying!"*, *"You worked so hard today!"*, and *"You kept at it and you did it!"*

Examples of what <u>not</u> to say when working with your child:

"Don't you remember (how to do this... what this is)....?"
"Why can't you get this?"
"We just did this yesterday, why don't you remember how?"
"I thought you'd know this by now."
"Suzie next door learned this a long time ago, you're getting behind."
"I don't have all day for you to learn this."
"It's so frustrating watching you struggle with this!"
"Johnnie knows how to do this already, when will you get it?"

"Just put it away, you're making too many mistakes."
"You're smarter than that."
"Come on, this isn't hard, you're not trying."

Positive phrases to use instead:

"That was great! Want to do it again?"
"You are so smart!"
"What would you like to do today?"
"Take your time; try it as much as you want."
"Don't worry; let's do something else today, ok?"
"Everyone makes mistakes when they're learning, you'll get it."
"Good job!"
"I like that!"
"Are you getting tired of this? We can always do it another day."
"Would you like to do this on your own now?"
"What do you like best about doing this?"
"You are doing really, really well!"

Use positive facial expressions. Smiling is always good. Put on a happy, amazed face when your child does something well. Offer immediate praise. Throw in lots of loving touches and hugs. The effect of these positive actions will be huge. They will outwardly reinforce your child's inner satisfaction at mastering new skills.

Encourage your child's efforts. Encouragement is non-judgmental feedback that focuses on effort and persistence, even in the face of mistakes. Your child will always make mistakes when using learning activities. Encouragement can make a positive out of this by pointing out that, *"You tried very hard and you didn't give up – that's great."* Or, *"Don't give up, try again."* This reinforces the value of **self-motivation and effort.**

Never miss a chance to encourage your child's efforts. The smallest improvements in muscle control, sensory awareness, reading and math skills, and gaining independence need to be recognized. Those little successes will add up to a child who expects to be successful in whatever she does – a powerful state of mind. A **positive self-image** is a primary benefit of learning activities.

Resources

Books by Maria Montessori

The Discovery of the Child

The Secret of Childhood

Spontaneous Activity In education

The Montessori Method

The Absorbent Mind

Great Blogs

Living Montessori Now

1+1+1=1

What DID We Do All Day?

The Education of Ours

Chasing Cheerios

Tot School

Discovery Moments

The Activity Mom

Carrots Are Orange

Mama Liberated

Peaceful Parenting

Counting Coconuts

The Home Teacher

Pink and Green Mama

Montessori MOMents

The Adventures of Bear

How We Montessori

The Hands On Homeschooler

Making Montessori Ours

No Time for Flash Cards

Teach Mama

Teach Preschool

Materials Online

MontessoriMom.com

Montessori Print Shop

Montessori For Everyone

Enchanted Learning

Montessori Outlet

montessorimaterials.org

Montessori Education

American Montessori Society

Montessoriconnections.com

Michaelolaf.net

montessori-ami.org

ourmontessorihome.com

Child Development

developingchild.harvard.edu

PBS Parents

washington.edu/earlychildhood

parents.com

naeyc.org

cfw.tufts.edu

childdevelopmentinfo.com

kidshealth.org

zerotothree.org

cdc.gov/ncbddd/actearly/index

whywaldorfworks.org/02_W_Education

Practical Life

Practical Life activities are the best first experiences for 2-5 year olds; and can be extended all the way into adulthood. Movement builds brain nerve pathways. Young children are eager to move and to learn to do things like pour, cut, sweep, polish, clean, prepare food, work fasteners, use simple tools, and all kinds of other things we do every day. They are programmed to want to function independently, to learn what we know, and to do what they see us doing.

> *"Imitation is the first instinct of the awakening mind."*
>
> **Maria Montessori**

Any daily task or activity you teach your preschooler to do becomes a Practical Life activity. **Take the time** to show your child how to do things around the house and you may be amazed at how well they do. Children do not have a bias about activities being chores or drudge work. They are thrilled to learn to do things they see adults doing but have not been allowed to do. These activities build **self-confidence** and a **positive self-image**. They allow children to be **participants** instead of just spectators.

By taking the next step and isolating experiences into **self-contained materials**, we allow children to focus on practicing the skills that will help them become independent. As they use these activities, they develop muscle control and coordination, especially in their hands and fingers. This leads directly into developing a proper writing grasp (p.60, 153). All these activities will focus your child's concentration and stimulate millions of new brain nerve connections and pathways.

> *"Do not tell them how to do it. Show them how to do it and do not say a word. If you tell them, they will watch your lips move. If you show them, they will want to do it themselves.*
>
> **Maria Montessori**

Here are examples of activities your child can learn to do at home:

Opening and closing doors, cupboards	Straightening a picture on the wall	Sticking on a stamp or sticker
Opening and closing lids, boxes, trunks, windows	Organizing a drawer	Lifting, carrying, and putting down a chair
Folding clothing	Hanging clothes on a hanger & with a clothespin	Handing someone scissors or a knife safely
Operating curtains and blinds	Using an egg whisk & an egg beater	Hanging a towel on a rack neatly
Sorting silverware	Offer a visitor a seat, something to drink	Adjusting bath water temperature
Polishing furniture, metal	Making an apology	Washing body and hair
Making the bed	Braiding yarn, ribbon, hair	Learning location of neighbor safe houses
Putting on a pillowcase	Brushing, feeding, bathing the dog	Vacuuming
Answering the phone	Using tablet apps	Checking items to make a shopping list
Location of fire extinguishers	Putting on a seatbelt	How to call 911
Finding weeds in the lawn and digging them out	Learning address and phone number	Drying and stacking dishes
Raking leaves	Fastening & unfastening jewelry clasps	Locking and unlocking doors
Turning on the computer	Wet mopping the floor	Using a cell phone
Opening & using favorite activity internet sites	Watering plants	Making a sandwich
Watching for dangers in traffic	Stop & look both ways before crossing the street	Sorting trash for recycling
Cleaning the car	Using a screwdriver, pliers	Tying shoelaces

Almost any daily life activity your child can safely learn to do is a Practical Life activity. The home is the natural place to learn these things. They are part of your daily life, readily available, and your child can use new skills in real life right away. Spills and mistakes are expected when learning to do new things. Always show your child how to clean up, and make this a natural part of every activity you can. Learning to clean up and take responsibility builds brain nerve pathways in the same way doing the activity does.

Practical Life activities combine movement, concentration, purposeful action, sense experiences, succeeding at challenging tasks, and fun. They build strong brain architecture and a positive, confident self-image.

The Jobs Jar

When your child learns how to do something, such as a task listed on page 57, write it down on a slip of paper. Put all these in a jar. Include some fun things like, "**Sing a little of your favorite song**", "**Hop to the door**", and "**Look outside until you find a bug.**" When your child is looking for something to do, have him draw slips out of the jar.

Free Play Tub

Pour white and brown rice into a plastic storage tub to a depth of about an inch. Add measuring spoons and a small measuring cup, small cups with and without handles, a little paint palette tray with depressions, and perhaps some coins and a few small animal figures, toy cars, etc. Let your child freely explore with the tub. You can use shredded paper, beans, dry corn, foam pom poms, colored gravel, and many other materials as filler. Hiding specific numbers of identical objects or bottle caps with the numerals 0-10 on them and counting or arranging them as they are found becomes a math activity. Do the same with simple words, starting with your child's name, printed on small cards. With the lid on tight, the tub can stay on your child's shelves. Free play tubs can become **Sensory Bins** when your child is ready. See page 78.

Encourage your child to count scoops as she spoons material into cups, and to try to pour right into the center of containers without spilling any material. When spills happen, show her how to stop right away and clean up. This is an essential part of using early learning materials.

Rolling a mat

The first step in the **Activity Cycle** (p. 28) is to create a work space with a small floor rug or table mat. Rolling and unrolling these can be an activity in itself, and is a nice way to reinforce the Activity Cycle. Demonstrate slowly, showing your child how to keep the ends even. This takes practice, that's the point. Young children actually enjoy learning to move with precision and control. They can get frustrated when things don't go their way, but practicing and eventually succeeding is what it's all about.   *Photo: Nursery Rhymes and Fun Times*

Transfers

Transfers involve moving materials back and forth between different containers. This may seem odd to parents accustomed to seeing children only playing with toys; but kids really get into it. They get to use cups, spoons, tongs, tweezers, and other tools. They experience the satisfaction of learning to pour their own drinks, serve themselves food, and use simple kitchen tools. They refine their hand grasp to eventually execute a **proper writing grasp**. If the timing is right, this will happen just about the time a child gets interested in writing letters and numbers. For such simple activities, transfers are excellent early childhood materials.

Above: three starter transfer activities, shown in order of difficulty going left to right. **Left:** moving water back and forth between two bowls using a small sponge cut from a larger one. **Middle:** rice is poured between two plain cups, sized small to fit a child's hand. **Right:** plastic kitchen tongs are used to move lightweight plastic practice golf balls around in the depressions of an egg carton. Using salt or water will add to the challenge in the middle activity.

With a 2-3 year old, start with the sponging activity and proceed to the next two when your child is ready, with plenty of practice at each step. Demonstrate each transfer first, and always spill a little water and rice and show your child how to clean up. When your child is good at pouring the rice without spilling, use salt, then water or syrup. Mastering the tongs requires opposing the thumb to all four fingers, the first step toward developing a proper writing grasp (illustration below).

Before your child starts using the more difficult transfers above, let her practice pouring rice, then water, back and forth between **measuring cups with handles and lips**. After this (left above), show your child how to use tweezers to move foam pom poms or beans between shot glasses or other small containers. Middle above: colored water is moved between the same cups using an eyedropper. At right, the smallest measuring spoon is used to move small beans between condiment cups.

In addition to learning to pour and use simple tools, the fine motor goal of transfers is developing a **proper writing grasp**, shown at left. This takes time and lots of practice, so make sure your child has easy access to these materials.

The Education of Ours

This tweezer transfer has exactly as many pom poms as there are suction cups on the soap holder. This teaches the critical math concept of **1:1 Correspondence**. You can use materials for putting lids on jars, 12 plastic eggs in an egg carton, and similar materials to teach 1:1 correspondence and encourage your child to practice counting. Both are great preparation for starting the Math Sequence activities starting on page 131. Put it all on a nice tray.

Playdough

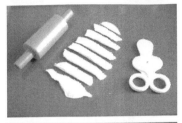

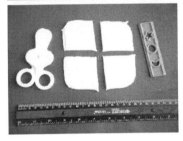

Every preschooler needs to have playdough handy. You can make your own, but the original is sold everywhere, inexpensive, and comes in cool sets with fun tools for cutting and rolling. Free play rolling, squeezing, and pounding is always fun. Mix colors to create wonderful effects. Roll similar sized balls in the same color for counting practice. Roll a sheet and let your child practice cutting it with scissors – playdough is easier to cut than paper. Help your child roll out 'snakes' and cut them into graded sizes – 1", 2", 3", etc.-and line them up. Roll sheets and cut them out in circles, triangles, rectangles, etc., to introduce shapes. Roll out a sheet, cut a square out of it with a box or food container lid, and show your child how to cut it in halves, thirds, and fourths for fractions practice. Check online for more fun playdough activities.

Montessori At Home! photos

Early Learning in the Kitchen

Your kitchen is a learning center. Practical life, sensory, science, fun times – it's all in your kitchen waiting for you and your child. Start by involving your child in every way you can, starting with tasks she can do now and adding more as she grows. Pouring, mixing, slicing, setting the table, washing up, it's all good.

Photo: sorting silverware at Chasing Cheerios

Teach hand washing early and often. Hands are the most common way infections spread. Use antimicrobial soap and show your child how to rub every surface with good friction for at least 20 seconds. *Shutterstock photo*

If you reorganize and place plates, cups, and utensils on low shelves, your child can get things out himself, which increases his independence. Get a small rolling pin and cookie cutters, small kitchen tools like spoons, whisk, ladle, tongs, and a child sized dustpan and hand broom. These are also used for Transfer activities (p. 59-60). Check out the **For Small Hands**, and **Montessori Services** web sites for these.

Maintain safety first. Make sure your kitchen has **GFI outlets**. Do not allow your child to use any tool or do any task which she cannot do safely. Be especially careful around the oven. Keep any eye out for fingers near doors and drawers. Some tasks will have to wait until your child is older.

Sensory experiences are everywhere in the kitchen. Tastes, smells, textures, sounds of tools and appliances, slimy eggs and oil, clouds of flour. Find all the ways possible to help your child touch, smell, taste, see, and hear new things when you cook. *Shutterstock photo*

Introduce new **language.** Talk about colors, names of ingredients, where they come from (find on Google Earth), names of kitchen tools, cooking terms, anything you can think of. Do internet searches of food items. Make name cards and labels for drawers, food containers, ingredients, tools.

Bring in **mathematics**. Count scoops, spoonfuls, cookies on a baking sheet, and plates on the table. Talk about fractions when cutting fruits. Explore the marks on the measuring cup, even if your child does not know what they mean yet.

Get everyone involved. Parents with an older and younger child often struggle to find appropriate activities each can do at the same time. Cooking projects can be perfect for this. Each child can handle tasks they are capable of. The results bring a cooperative sense of accomplishment. Positive shared experiences help balance out the sibling issues that many families experience. Here are examples of more things your child can do in the kitchen:

Practical Life

pouring	cutting & slicing	rolling & kneading flour
juicing	making toast	loading dishwasher
crack eggs	cookie cutting	tossing salad
spreading with a knife	grinding spices & nuts	whisking & mixing
using a spatula	shelling nuts	using tongs

Sensory

spice smells	crush grapes	adjust water temperature
feel vegetables	slimy eggs	tasting
food & juice colors	cold of the freezer	weight of vegetables
textures of everything	cooking smells	sounds of food prep

Science

frozen water expands	yeast rising in bread	water to ice to gas
salt dissolving in water	taste buds on tongue	sprouting beans
water boiling point	measuring temperatures	growing veggies

Mathematics

counting everything	measuring cups, spoons	groups of objects
weighing items	addition, subtraction	planning a table setting
cutting geometric shapes	following a recipe	fractions cutting fruit

Language

recipes

ingredients

talking about food

food labels

food terms

names of foods

boxes

starting & ending sounds

You can easily create self-contained learning materials around a kitchen theme. At left, a child scoops balls from a piece of watermelon onto a plate and inserts a toothpick in each for serving. Use a plastic placemat work area, a nice plate, and a little cup for the toothpicks.

Counting Coconuts

Set up an activity to practice cutting with a banana, cutting board, plastic knife, and a small plate. Show your child how to peel the banana and cut slices, then let her take over. After cutting, she can serve banana pieces to the family and then clean up.

Similar materials can easily be made up to pit cherries, spread peanut butter on crackers, make peanut butter logs with celery, all kinds of things.

Fabric Folding

Get a pack of washcloths and draw lines on them as shown below using a ruler and marker. Put them in a nice basket. Show your child how to carefully fold along the lines, and let him take over. This is a great activity for learning about shapes, while also developing fine motor control of the hand and finger muscles. *Tot School Photo*

Cleaning a Table

Discovery Moments

A bucket with a sponge, soap, brush, and towel makes a table washing material. Help your child the first time to get water in the bucket, get the table soapy, scrub it, and sponge and towel it clean. Then do the chairs. Kids love the process of this activity, and learn a sense of responsibility.

Open & Close

Counting Coconuts

Collect identical glass jars of different sizes with lids. Put the lids in a little bag and put everything in a basket. Your child will get practice estimating and matching sizes, and fine motor work learning to screw and unscrew the lids. Extend the material by using various sized little boxes and other containers with lids.

Marbles & Golf Tees

Pink & Green Mama

Put colorful marbles and golf tees in a bowl. Get thick floral foam for anchoring flowers, and put it all on a tray. Show your child how to push the tees in and place marbles on them. Let her explore freely. When she gets the tees in straight and the marbles stay on, show her how to make a line of tees. Introduce counting as up to 10 tees are placed in line. Use ping pong balls for a new challenge. Write the numbers 0-10 on the balls and tees for a numeral matching activity. Line them up **left to right to prepare for reading**.

Threading, Lacing, Weaving, Sewing

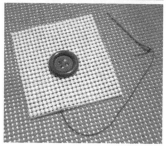

Children love the sequential movements and results of these materials. For younger children, start with large wood beads on a shoestring. Use smaller beads as finger control improves (top). Count the beads. Make control patterns by coloring in rows of circles on paper and have your child match the pattern with the beads. Use the 'shapes' feature on your word processor and print out large geometric shapes on card stock (second photo). Punch holes around the edges and show your child how to lace through the holes. Tie them together to make a mobile. Make name labels for the shapes to introduce new language. Start weaving by weaving a ribbon through the rows of a dish drying rack or laundry basket (third photo). Next, make notches on opposite edges of a small Styrofoam dish or a piece of cardboard. Wrap yarn around to make the **warp**. Cut a **shuttle** from cardboard and attach the **woof** yarn to weave through the warp threads (fourth photo). When your child has sufficient finger control skills, cut 4" squares of grid pattern shelf liner. Get a pack of child's safety sewing needles and some large, colorful buttons. Show your child how to sew a button onto a square of material, then let him work at it. It will take some practice, and that's the idea. Later, your child can sew buttons onto felt with a real needle, with close supervision.

Cutting & Slicing

Left: *Montessori MOMents.* Top right: *Peaceful Parenting.* Bottom right: *The Activity Mom*

Start scissor cutting practice with a sheet of play doh, which is easier to cut than paper (top left). Always have your child keep his **thumb up, like shaking hands**. When she is ready, give her 1" wide strips of paper to freely cut pieces from. Next, add vertical lines and numbers (top right) and show your child how to cut along the lines while counting the numbers. Finally, print out large geometric shapes and let your child practice cutting curved and straight sided figures (bottom right).

Above left: a toddler can practice slicing with a dull kitchen or plastic knife and a banana. Later, make a self-contained material for banana cutting (right above). Try cheese slicing next.   *Left: Chasing Cheerios photo*

Above are more challenging, self-contained materials. At left, peeling and slicing carrots. At right, slicing eggs with an egg slicer. Can you think of more? *Counting Coconuts photos*

Flower Arranging

Use a selection of real or artificial flowers and a jar or vase, all on a tray with scissors. If your child needs help, poke holes in the jar lid to guide the flower stems, as in the photo. Later, she can freely arrange the flowers herself.

Discovery Moments photo

Building a Flashlight

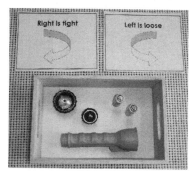

Turn something we do without thinking into a learning activity. Put a disassembled flashlight and the batteries on a tray. Show your child how to put it together and screw the top on and off. *"Right is tight, left is loose"*. If needed, make up cards as in the photo with arrows showing that right is tight, left is loose.

Nuts, Bolts, & Screws

Nuts and bolts provide excellent hand and finger control and coordination practice. Start (top) with a simple 2 – compartment tray or just a little box with different sizes of bolts and one nut for each. Help your child learn that right is tight and left is loose. Another good activity (second photo) uses bolts in these diameters: ¼", 3/8". ½", 7/16", and 5/8". Each bolt should be just long enough to hold 5 washers and a nut screwed on tight. This will create a line of bolts that get shorter after they are all put together. You can also find good plastic nuts and bolts sets, like the **Ryan's Room Creative Big Nuts & Bolts** set (third photo).

Using T-nuts, a nut driver tool, and a set of nut drivers (fourth photo down), you can make a board like the one the boy in the bottom photo is using. Get a nice piece of finished plywood about a foot square. Drill holes for the T-nuts, then hammer them in. Get various sizes to match the bolts you buy. Now your child can practice matching up the bolts to the proper T-nuts and turn them in tight.

Extend your child's new skills by showing her how to tighten drawer knobs by holding the screw from turning using a screwdriver inside the drawer front while turning the drawer pull to the right. Tighten handles with 2 screws from inside the drawer with a screwdriver.

Hammering

L: *Chasing Cheerios* **M:** *Fresh Idea Mama* **R:** *Little Schoolhouse in the Suburbs*

Have your child wear safety goggles, as the golf tees and nails might jump around. Start with a wooden mallet, golf tees, and a piece of floral foam. When your child is ready, use a meat softening mallet to pound tees into a box filled with compressed newspaper. At right above: golf tees hammered into playdough compressed into little baking pans. Help your child learn to hammer real nails by pre-drilling wood blocks with holes that allow the nails to be inserted about halfway. This makes it less likely that off-center hammer blows will bend the nails, strike a finger, or that the 'nails' might jump up.

Materials like the **Hammering Shapes** at **For Small Hands** use a corkboard and little brads to hammer the shapes to the board. These are great for hammering and exploring how shapes can fit together to make new shapes.

Mama Liberated

Dressing

"If teaching is to be effective with young children, it must assist them to advance on the way to independence. We must help them learn to walk without assistance, to run, to go up and down stairs, to pick up fallen objects, to dress and undress, to wash themselves, to express their needs in a way that is clearly understood, and to attempt to satisfy their desires through their own efforts. All this is part of an education for independence."

Maria Montessori, *The Discovery of the Child*

Start with a simple basket of loose fitting clothes your child can practice getting on and off. Avoid rushed mornings and look for quiet times when you and your child can explore with these clothes in an unhurried way. Work with one clothing item at a time. Socks are a good place to start, pants can come next. Start with **loose, simple clothing,** like elastic waist pants, shorts, and skirts; t-shirts one size too big, socks with heels so it is easy to orient them. Let your child work on fastener skills as activities in themselves (keep reading) before she tries to button suspenders or shirts, pants with zippers, or tie her shoes.

Velcro
Zippers (pants)
Snaps
Buttons
Buckles
Zippers (coats)
Shoelaces

At left is a sequence of dressing challenges in a rough order of difficulty. Old purses are great for fasteners practice. You can drape coats, sweaters, and shirts over a chair and sit your child facing the back of the chair to practice zippering, snapping, and buttoning. For shoelaces, check You Tube for videos of the 'Bunny Ears' and traditional methods. Choose one and give your child an old shoe to use for practice to remove the stress of trying to tie shoes when you are headed out the door.

Locks, Latches, & Keys

The simple tray at top left has wooden rings, locks, and keys. Add a combination lock and a cable lock for more challenge. The bottom photo shows a camera bag that has zipper, velcro, and snap closures. A combination lock has been locked over the strap. Inside are a keyed padlock, colorful snap links, and screw links for different kinds of fine motor challenges.

Top: Family Go Simple

Care of Self

The drive toward independence finds a natural outlet in learning to perform personal care tasks. Children readily learn these skills with a little instruction and demonstration.

Bathing

Safety Note: **Young children must be supervised continuously in the bathtub. Children can drown in very little water**. Have everything you need by the tub before drawing the bath water. With guidance, a young child can learn how to put soap on a washcloth and clean themselves. Encourage them to reach every spot they can. Shampooing usually requires assistance until a child is about 6 or so; but younger children can start learning how and help with rinsing and drying. Make bath time a warm, inviting, and fun experience.

Using a faucet

Let your child practice filling a small cup by creating a moderate flow of water, fast enough to fill the cup fairly quickly, but not so fast that it splashes all over the counter. You will need to provide a small stepstool at the faucets you want your child to be able to use independently. Let your child turn on the hot water, feel how it warms up, and learn to adjust the temperature. **Safety Note**: **Keep the heat setting on your water heater low enough to prevent scalding. This is usually around 120°F.**

Hand washing

Frequent hand washing is the primary weapon in preventing infections. **More infections are spread by the hands than by any other route**. Provide antibacterial hand soap in a pump container at every sink in your home. Remind your child to immediately wash her hands upon returning home from any trip – especially after a trip to the store. Show your child how to use lukewarm water and soap; and how to rub her hands together with moderate friction for at least 30 seconds, washing every hand and finger surface well. Show your child how to dry his hands properly and throw the towel away.

Oral care

Establishing good habits of brushing and flossing are essential elements of personal hygiene. Make this fun and participate in helping your child learn these skills. Let your child try out a few different tooth brushes and good toothpastes to find his favorites. Make sure your child has regular teeth brushing and flossing times every day, especially after meals. Electric toothbrushes clean teeth better than non-electric. There are many inexpensive models for kids available. There are many web sites and videos that will help your child learn the hows and whys of tooth care.

Plaque disclosing tablets are wonderful for demonstrating to children the importance of brushing properly and keeping their teeth clean. The experiences of seeing the plaque on their teeth stained blue or red, and brushing properly to get it off, make big impressions on young children. For a downloadable PDF chart showing how to brush and floss teeth, visit: **mycohi.org**

Coughing

Show your child how to cough into an elbow, as coughing into the hands covers them with microorganisms. Coughing accompanied by colored mucous and a fever usually means a trip to the doctor. A chronic cough in a young child is always a cause for concern and evaluation by a physician.

Grace & Courtesy

Learning good manners and basic social skills is an essential part of early childhood education. Children will not learn to respect the rights, abilities, and value of other people if they are not taught how to interact with others in a civilized way. The earlier you teach your child these social skills, the better.

Remind your child to say **please and thank you**. Establish natural consequences if the words are not used – such as the thing the child wants not being produced! Use these words yourself all the time.

Stand between your child and something he wants, and have him practice saying, "*Excuse me,*" as you move aside. If your child wants to talk to you when you or someone else is talking, always emphasize that he must wait for a break in the conversation and then say, "*Pardon me,*" rather than simply interrupt. Practice this at home and when shopping or in other social situations.

Do more role playing practice with your child. Pretend you are someone else and teach your child how to introduce herself to you, using her full name. Show her how to greet someone you meet. Help him learn to make requests, such as "*Please pass the salt.*" "*May I please use that when you're done?*" Help your child learn how to properly phrase requests to others. Practice making requests back and forth with your child.

At the store or any public venue where people are moving in a space, indicate to your child when she should step aside to allow other people to move by. Teach your child to observe others and see when he is about to bump into someone or block someone's path. This helps young children begin to recognize that they live in world with other people; and that they must responsibly share space with them.

Learning how to **sit quietly** is an essential skill. You can practice by setting up a stopwatch or watching the second hand on an analog clock and making a game out of remaining silent and still for a period of time. As your child improves, the time can be extended. You may find it beneficial for both you and your child to try simple **mindfulness meditation**, such as being aware your own breathing. This 'attentive relaxation' has been shown to boost brain power and reduce stress. It is not hard and is not a religious activity. You simply pay attention to your breathing and watch the movements of your mind. This can help you and your child relax while you each learn more about how your minds work.

Extending Practical Life Activities

Mastering the skills of daily life should not stop when your child reaches six. Simply increase the challenges and continue teaching your child how to do things for herself. Young children should learn early on that being part of a family means sharing the work of keeping the home and cars clean, shopping, food preparation, taking out the trash, doing the laundry, etc. A reasonable list of chores is a great way for a child to learn responsibility. There is no need to pay children for this.

Yard work and gardening are fantastic Practical Life activities. Young children can dig up weeds and water plants. Gardening allows a child to learn the life cycle of plants and grow food to eat as well as colorful flowers and beautiful ground covers. Your child can plant her own plants and care for them. Don't be afraid to let your child use his muscles to carry bags of soil and other things. Outdoor family projects can be wonderful bonding and learning experiences.

As children get older they can learn to use hand tools to make basic repairs, to paint, to change light bulbs – all kinds of things. Learning to play a musical instrument is a wonderful activity. Playing music has a direct positive effect on a child's intelligence and intellectual ability in other areas of study.

Get your child involved early in the daily life activities that make the world go around and he will develop a positive and confident self-image, learn responsibility, acquire muscle control and coordination, build strong brain architecture, and gain an understanding of how our world works on a daily basis. Nice!

"The real preparation for education is the study of oneself. The training of the teacher....is something far more than a learning of ideas. It includes the training of character; it is a preparation of the spirit."

Maria Montessori

Sensorial

We interpret information from our five senses in our brains. Sensory inputs open brain nerve pathways in young children. These activities also encourage children to **focus attention** on the sensory characteristics of objects: visual appearance, dimensions, textures, weight, color, relative size, smells, tastes, and sounds. They involve children in making **purposeful decisions** based on sensory information. Your child will focus on one or more senses to identify largest and smallest; make gradations by size and shades of color; and match objects by sound, smell, taste, and touch. This decision-making activity helps establish new brain nerve pathways. Young children who do these activities find learning math and reading much easier. They develop the visual acuity and discrimination that, combined with the confidence and hand and finger control gained by using Practical Life materials, enable a child to easily master letters and numbers. Besides being great fun, **Practical Life and Sensorial materials set the stage for everything that follows**. When a child starts using Sensorial materials, it is usually time to start a slow, gradual introduction to high quality **digital tablet apps**. Examples are recommended starting in this section and throughout the rest of the book. Read more on page 106.

"The mind of a little child is certainly not a blank when he begins the education of the senses, but his concepts are all confused. He begins to distinguish various traits in objects already known. He distinguishes quantity from quality and separates form from color. He distinguishes dimensions in objects that are long or short, thick or thin, large or small. He separates colors into groups and calls them by name. He notices the varying intensities of colors, calling the two extremes light and dark. Finally, he distinguishes tastes from smells, lightness from softness, and sounds from noises. He succeeds through the education of his senses in ordering his mental images. This is the first act of ordering in his developing mind. This sense of order that has been acquired early is of utmost importance for later life."

Maria Montessori, *The Discovery of the Child*

Sorting

Sorting activities are versatile, excellent sensory experiences. Children are attracted to sorting various objects based on their characteristics. They get to create order out of chaos while learning a lot about the sensory qualities of various materials. In the top photo, 4 kinds of **pasta** pieces are sorted by shape from a central bowl into 4 smaller condiment cups. This is a good basic design for many sorting materials, like the one in the second photo, in which 7 colors of small **wooden beads** are sorted by picking them up with kitchen tongs. This adds a fine motor control element to the material. The next photo shows a bowl of **coins** - pennies, nickels, dimes, and quarters - being sorted.

It is easy to add new challenges. The fourth photo down shows cut straws being sorted by length. Cut some in 3, 5, and 7" lengths to start. Add more lengths of straws with less difference between them later. In the bottom photo, a sorting activity encourages counting. Five colors of beads are included: one of one color, two of the next, three of the next, and so on. As the child sorts, mathematical groups are created, encouraging counting.

Many materials can be used for sorting. Here are a few examples:

colored paper clips	colored rubber bands	beans
Buttons of different sizes and colors	Pom poms with tweezers	m&m candies

Sorting Images

When your child has had practice sorting three dimensional objects, start using **images**. At left is a Land – Water – Air sorting activity with photos from the internet of fish, boats, birds, airplanes, cars, mammals, etc. Put name cards at the top saying '**Land**', '**Water**', and '**Air**' in a typestyle similar to that shown here, which will match the Sandpaper Letters you will be using soon (p. 153). Other image sorting options:

living & non-living	insect, mammal, fish, bird, crustacean	modes of transportation
types of fruits & vegetables	straight sided, curved sided objects	types of clouds

Sorting Apps

iTunes has a number of good sorting apps, including:

Sort It Out   **Simple Sort**   **Smart Fish: Magic Matrix**

Sensory Bins

A Sensory Bin is a tub or other large container with various materials in it for a child to freely handle and explore with. Above are samples.

At left is a bin for a younger child with rice, pasta, and plastic cookie cutter shapes. You could add other items, such as large, colored wooden beads (watch for small objects with children under 3), cotton balls, etc. In the middle is a beach themed bin with sand, sea shells, a plastic turtle and little people in beach attire. At right is a Christmas theme bin with cotton ball 'snow', jingle bells, little wrapped packages containing surprises, and snowflakes cut from card stock. Search 'Sensory Bin' online for more ideas. With the lid on tight, your child's favorite bins are always ready for use.

Extend Sensory Bin activities by burying bottle caps with the numerals 0-10 on them for your child to find and identify. You can also hide slips of paper with meaningful words – the names of your family members, the names of colors, etc. Bury plastic dinosaurs in a dirt bin for your budding archeologist to dig out and discover.

Colors

Most young children today are aware early on of the Primary Colors: **red**, **yellow**, and **blue**, and the Secondary Colors: **orange**, **green**, and **purple**, and they also often know **brown**, **grey**, **pink**, **white**, and **black**. Teaching your child these colors and names can easily be done using paint sample cards from the hardware store and **Three Step Lessons** (p. 35). Start with the Primary colors and do 3 at a time until your child knows all the above colors. Set the paint sample cards out and have your child find objects in your home in all the colors. Point out these colors whenever you can until your child has them down. Search **You Tube** for videos for kids about colors, and get the free **Colors iPad app** if you like.

Color Mixing

Once your child knows the Primary colors, this is a fun activity. Get a plastic mat, plastic ice cube tray, a couple of eyedroppers, a measuring cup, a cleanup sponge, and red, yellow, and blue food coloring.

1. Set the tray horizontally on the mat in front of your child.
2. Your child fills the measuring cup half full with water and then fills each section of the tray half full with water.
3. Your child adds a few drops of blue food coloring to the top left section of the tray. In the next section to the right, he adds a few drops of red, and in the next one to the right, a few drops of yellow. Show your child how to clean the eyedropper using clear water between colors.
4. Your child puts a few drops of blue from the first section into the fourth section down, then adds a few drops of yellow from the yellow section. Have him flush the eyedropper with clear water between colors. The fourth section will now have green water. Point out that, "*Blue plus yellow makes green.*"
5. In the fifth section down, your child mixes yellow and red to make orange. "*Yellow plus red makes orange.*"
6. In the sixth section down, your child mixes blue and red to make purple (or violet). "*Blue plus red makes purple.*"
7. Let your child freely explore mixing colors in the tray sections along the bottom.
8. When finished, your child can dump the tray water into a bucket and clean everything up for next time.

Color Shades

This activity requires good **visual discrimination**. If your child has a hard time with very similar shades, use every other shade at first so the differences between them are clearer and your child has quick success with the material. Success is key in early learning.

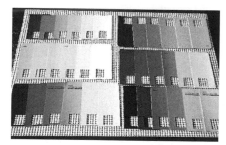

Collect paint sample cards that have multiple shades of a single color. The best have 3-5 shades on each card, so that two cards will give you 6-10 shades of one color, each shade slightly darker than the last. Try to get bold, clear colors. Cut out all the separate colors and keep each color set together with a rubber band. Put them all in a little bowl or box. Invite your child to do a new activity and have him lay out a work mat or floor rug.

Let your child pick a set of one color, and have her lay out the cards in that set at random on the rug. Ask, *"Can you find the darkest one?"* Help only as or if needed. Your child places the darkest shade on the left side of the mat. Now ask, *"Can you find the darkest one of those that are left?"* Your child places this one to the right of the darkest shade. Continue until all the cards are in a line from darkest to lightest going left to right. Repeat with more colors as long as your child wants to.

Setting things up to go left to right prepares a child for reading.

Pattern Matching

When your child has colors down pretty well, try this. Save fruit juice concentrate lids or similar lids. Get a variety of paper in colorful patterns from a crafts store. Cut circles to fit the lids and glue them on, making 2 lids of each pattern. Have your child lay them out at random and match them up.

Laura Ingalls Wannabe

Good early iPad apps for developing visual skills include:

Photo Touch Food
I Tot Cards
Memory King
Kids Can Match – Animals

Dimensional Materials

Three dimensional materials provide hands-on experience with shapes and forms. This is how young children learn about spatial relationships, size variations, angles and edges, and geometry. They also exercise their creativity and improve sensory acuity and discrimination. Montessori called this the *"Education of the senses."* The activities shown here are a mix of homemade and commercial materials. Together with the Practical Life materials, these experiences are the heart of early childhood education.

There are many good commercial dimensional materials, including:

Inchimals	**Guidecraft Nesting Sort & Stack Cubes and Cylinders**
Melissa & Doug Wooden Animal Nesting Blocks	**Melissa & Doug Geometric Stacker**
Lego building sets	**Brio building sets**
Wooden blocks	**Goobi Magnets**

Montessori Dimensional Materials

These materials have been used for over a hundred years, and are still fascinating to children today. They give a child hands-on experiences with relative size and gradations, shapes, and geometry. They are designed to auto-educate, meaning children get what they need simply by handling and playing with them. These can all be found online at suppliers like Montessori Outlet.

At the top is the **#1 Knobbed Cylinder Block**. This and the **#3 block** are the most useful for the home, usually for 2-3 year olds. The second photo shows the **Knobless Cylinders**, used by 2-5 year olds. Next is the classic **Pink Tower**, which 2-4 year olds typically find irresistible. There are 10 cubes, from 1 centimeter to 10 centimeters. Next down are the **Red Rods**. These 10 rectangular prisms get larger in 10 centimeter increments, from 10cm to the longest at 1 meter. These are pretty large for home use, and alternatives are given. The bottom photo shows the **Brown Stair**, 10 rectangular prisms that get thicker by 1 centimeter each from 1 centimeter thick to 10 centimeters.

At left: the **Geometric Solids**. These are cool wooden shapes that teach a child about geometry by being handled. Put them in a nice basket. The next photo shows the **Mystery Bag with Geometric Shapes**. These are smaller, hand size shapes in pairs, along with a couple of nice drawstring bags that can be used for many activities involving the **stereognostic sense**, the ability to determine shape by feel alone. You can do activities with all kinds of objects using the mystery bags, and they are inexpensive, so these are a must-have material for your home preschool.

Photos: Montessori Outlet

Presenting the Montessori Dimensional Materials

Montessori schools have detailed presentations for these materials. At home, have your child create a work space, show her how to handle each material with care and respect, and let her work with them as long as she wants to. Children will discover how to make a tower and lay out the Red Rods and Brown (or Broad) Stair in graduated patterns, as in the photos. This is more meaningful than if we simply show them. Auto-education is the goal here. It is very helpful to use **new language** terms when your child uses the materials. *Largest / smallest, longest / shortest, widest / narrowest, larger than / smaller than, points, corners, edges, faces, straight sided, curved*, etc., are all terms to introduce. The names of the Geometric Solids can be taught using **Three Step Lessons** (p. 35). You should also **make name cards** for them. They are:

Cube	Sphere	Rectangular Prism
Ovoid	Ellipsoid	Cylinder
Cone	Triangular Prism	Square Based Pyramid
	Triangular Based Pyramid	

If your child needs some help after a time to make, say, the Pink Tower, show him how by asking him to find the *largest* cube and set it aside. Now, ask, *"Can you find the largest one of those that are left?"* Have him find that one and place it on top of the largest cube. Continue until the tower is built. This can easily be done with the rods and stair also, looking for the shortest rod each time and lining up all their left ends; and looking for the thickest stair each time and lining them up as in the photo. The materials can also be used together to make all kinds of new constructions.

Counting is easily introduced. Montessori made many materials with ten objects to help children in counting to ten and making groups of up to ten objects. This is the foundation for the ten-based Mathematics materials that come later. Encourage your child to count the cylinders, cubes and rods. Talk with your child about which objects have straight sides and which have curved sides. Help your child discover objects in your home and city that have geometric shapes. Search the geometric shapes online for images of more objects.

The Mystery Bag with Geometric Shapes

The **Mystery Bag** (p. 83) has two of each geometric shape and two bags. Put one set in each bag. Take a shape from one bag, show it to your child, and have her find it by feel in the other bag. This can be done using two each of almost any common small items that will fit in the bag: coins, washers, pasta shapes, small toy animals and other toy figures.

Have your child place the Geometric Solid name cards on a rug or mat, and put 3 shapes in the bag at a time. Your child feels the shapes and states which one each is before pulling each one out of the bag and placing it under the correct name card. You can do this with quarters, nickels, pennies, and dimes. Make name cards and let your child decide which coin each one is before pulling them out of the bag and placing them under the name cards for the coins. Place a number of identically sized legos in the bag and ask your child to connect 2, then 4, then 3, then 6, etc., of them together and bring them out to count and check.

Using Control Images

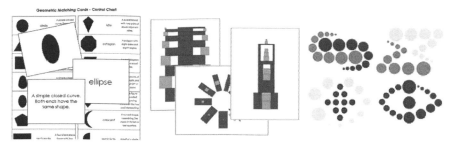

Montessori Print Shop is an online source for printable materials. Above are just a few: the **Geometric Matching Cards, Pink Tower and Broad Stair Patterns**, and **Knobless Cylinder Pattern Cards**. If you get the Montessori dimensional materials, these printables are very helpful in encouraging your child's development of **abstract thought** (p. 14). The Knobless Cylinders, for example, are placed on their matching images on the control card. It is also simple to make your own pattern cards. Take a look at the many printables available from Montessori Print Shop. Using your color printer it is as easy as click – print – teach.

(The primary purpose of the Sensorial materials is that), *"...The child train himself to observe; that he be led to make comparisons between objects, to form judgments, to reason, and to decide."*

Quote in italics: Maria Montessori, *Dr. Montessori's Own Handbook*

Left & Middle: *Discovery Moments*   Right: *The Education of Ours*

If the Red Rods are too long for your home, make a smaller set.

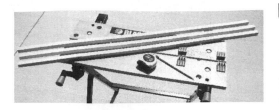 

Get three straight, 5/8" X 36" long, poplar crafts wood rods. Poplar cuts and sands easily. Saw carefully to make 10 rods. The first will be 1" long, the next 2", the next 3", the next 4", etc., up to the last rod at 10" long. Sand them smooth without taking too much wood off, and paint them primary red. You could also use straight 3/4" wooden doweling.

Binomial and Trinomial Cubes

These Montessori materials are Math materials for older children, and very cool Sensorial materials for 3-6 year olds. The **Binomial Cube** (top) shows the binomial theorem in three dimensions. The **Trinomial Cube** (bottom), shows the trinomial theorem in three dimensions. Don't ask me to explain the math!

Montessori schools have lengthy presentations for these materials. At home, a simpler approach works just as well. 3-4 year olds start out with the Binomial Cube. Late 4 to 6 year olds really enjoy the challenge of the Trinomial Cube.

A good presentation is to download the Binomial and Trinomial Cube Control Cards from Montessori Print Shop. Lay out the Binomial Cube Control Card, take a good look at how the cubes are arranged in the box, then start taking them out and placing them on their matching images.

Once all the blocks are on the card, they can be replaced in reverse order. The lids give you a guide as to where the blocks go. Remember: **larger blocks go on the bottom, and the colors on the blocks cover (match) the colors on the lid**. Search You Tube for good videos of demonstrating these materials to see how they are presented in Montessori schools.

Nuts, Washers, & Bolts

Hex bolts, **washers**, and **nuts** are great Sensorial dimensional materials for size grading, matching, and making designs. Store these materials in special containers that look inviting on your child's shelves. Get bolts, and the washers and nuts to fit them. These sizes work well:

3/4 X 3	**5/8 X 2 1/2**
1/2 X 2 1/4	**7/16 X 2**
3/8 X 1 ¾	**5/16 X 1 1/2**
1/4 X 1 1/4	**1/4 X 1**
1/4 X ¾	**1/4 X 1/2**

The hex bolts make a group of ten objects for size grading as with the Red Rods. Standing them on end and lining them up close together is a fine motor exercise. Let your child experiment making designs with the washers and nuts.

All these objects are great for counting and introducing terms like largest, smallest, larger than, smaller than, hexagonal, threads, and of course, bolts, washers, and nuts!

Plane Figures & Geometric Shapes

When your child has had experience manipulating three dimensional materials, introduce two dimensional plane figures and shapes. This is part of the progression into abstract thought (p. 14).

Left: Buy large buttons in different shapes. Trace them on paper, and your child can match the buttons to their outlines. You can use many different objects for tracing. **Middle**: Your child can make geometric shapes with rubber bands using a **Geo Board**. **Right**: **Melissa & Doug's Pattern Blocks** are a great material for making plane figures. There are control cards and printables online your child can use to create many images from these. **Good iPad apps include:**

Geo Board   **Mosaic HD**   **Pattern Blocks**   **My First Tangrams**

Montessori Blue Constructive Triangles

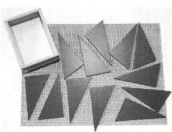

A set of 12 right angle triangles, available online for around $12. By putting triangles together, your child can make all kinds of basic geometric shapes, and more complicated constructions, including:

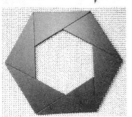  

Geometric shapes your child can make with the blue triangles include a square, rectangle, rhombus, and parallelogram. Can you find more? The **Geometric Cabinet Control Booklet** from **Montessori Print Shop** has many shapes for your child to learn. There are so many wonderful printables offered here that all parents doing learning activities at home need to check out this resource. A couple of good **iPad apps** for working with geometric shapes and plane figures are the **Geometric Cabinet App** by Rantek, and **My First 3D Puzzle: Animals. Puzzles** are good plane figure activities. Great ones can be found at Melissa & Doug's, and the **Mindware Pattern Play** (Amazon) is also excellent.

Memory Game

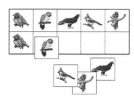

The Memory Game, formerly known on TV as 'Concentration', is a classic early childhood activity. A set of images are placed or printed onto cards, 2 cards for each image. All the cards are laid out in a grid pattern. The first player turns over a card, then another to try and match it. If no match, both cards are turned over and the second player takes a turn. As more cards are turned over, each player has a chance to remember where the cards are.

Eventually, a player makes a match, and those cards are removed from the game. This continues until all cards are matched. The winner has the most matches. The game is easily played solo, also. **Montessori Print Shop** has beautiful Memory Card games free for downloading. Free memory games online can be found at **The Kidz Page** and **PBSKids.org**. You can make your own memory game cards by printing out or gluing images on card stock to make any kind of game your child likes. Good **iPad memory game apps** include **Preschool Memory Match** and **Memory King**. Good **iPad apps** for learning ordering, visual, thinking, and language skills include:

Photo Touch Concepts	**Shapes Builder**
Little Solver Preschool Logic	**Pattern recognition Preschool**

Comparative Adjectives   Things That Go Together

Little Puzzles   Photo Touch Farm Animals

The Copy Me Tray

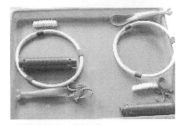

This cool activity comes courtesy of **The Activity Mom,** a great Mom blog. Get a large tray and a collection of **pairs** of identical objects. These can be almost anything, but there should be a variety of sizes and shapes. Embroidery hoops, eating utensils, pencils, napkins, cookie cutters, plastic fruit, party favors, and salt & pepper shakers are a few suggestions. Split the pairs up so that you and your child each have one set of the objects. Have your child close her eyes while you make a pattern using some of your objects on one side of the tray. Now, your child opens her eyes and sets up her objects to match yours. Switch roles and let your child go first. This is an excellent experience in visual discrimination and spatial awareness.

The Activity Mom photos

"What we need is a world full of miracles, like the miracle of the young child seeking work and independence, and manifesting a wealth of enthusiasm and love."

Maria Montessori

Touch

The following activities educate your child's sense of touch. It is important to allow children to touch things with a variety of textures. Place rocks, dry grasses, lace, glass, metal, ceramic, wooden, and various types of textiles around your home to give your child many touch experiences.

Tactile Qualities of Objects

Place objects with widely differing textures in a basket. Touch them with your child and talk about how each one feels. Use as much new language as possible to describe the touch sensations and naming the various materials. Include words such as, *hard, soft, rough, smooth, large, small, solid, spongy, firm, elastic, compressible, star-shaped, heart shaped, spherical, rubber, glass, fabric, tile, organic, inorganic, light, heavy, and square.* Take turns closing your eyes and trying to describe and identify objects the other person hands you. Try using a Mystery Bag (p. 83) or a blindfold, also.

Fabric Feel

This material is in every Montessori preschool. From old clothing or fabric store scraps, cut two 5" squares each of various fabrics. Get some that are similar, and some very different. Examples: nylon, lace, corduroy, denim, burlap, felt, cotton, vinyl, silk, and terrycloth. Place them in a basket, along with a **blindfold**.

Your child puts on the blindfold and holds out her hands. Put a fabric scrap in one of her hands for her to feel. Now, put a **very different feeling fabric** in her other hand, have her feel them both well, and ask, *"Do they feel the same, or different?"* If your child states they are the same or is not sure, have her take off the blindfold and see for herself. Play with the fabrics without the blindfold, talking about which feel the same and different so your child gets the idea. You can use the blindfold later or another day.

If your child states correctly that they are different, keep putting more fabrics in her second hand until she feels one and says it is the same as the first fabric you handed her. He can take off the blindfold to check. Continue this way until all the squares are matched. Be sure to switch roles and have your child hand you the fabrics.

Use as many new language terms as possible when doing the activity, including the names of the fabrics and their textures: rough, smooth, silky, ridges, patterns, thick, thin, etc.

Sandpaper Matching

This challenging activity for 4-6 yr. olds matches different grades of sandpaper by touch. Start with the roughest and smoothest grades and add the in between grades later. Write the grades of the sandpaper strips on the backs of the cards. This activity also prepares your child for using the **Sandpaper letters** (p. 153) and **numerals** (p. 133).

Cut two colors of bright card stock into 2X5" cards. Make 4 of each color.

From sandpaper sheets in 80, 100, 150, and 220 grit, cut two 1.5 X 4" strips of each grade.

Glue stick one of each sandpaper pair to one color of card, and the other to the other color, making four pairs. You will have an orange and a red card with 80 grit, another orange / red pair with 100 grit, etc.

Have your child close his eyes or put on a blindfold. Hand him a strip and have him feel it with the tips of his fingers. Now hand him different strips and ask. *"Do they feel the same or different?"* When he makes a match, have him check the numbers on the back to see if he matched the strips correctly. Wear the blindfold yourself and have your child hand you strips. This is a challenging activity, so be patient and positive.

Baric Touch

Baric means **weight**. This material for **4-6 yr. olds** helps a child to sense and compare the **weight** of objects by holding them in her hands. This material also quantifies weight differences and introduces math using **quarters**, **clear plastic mini-cups** (useful, cheap little cups with lids), and a **blindfold**. You will know quickly if the material is appropriate for your child's current abilities.

Lay out 8 cups (photo).

Have your child count out 1 quarter into each of two cups. Help your child if needed to write the numeral 1 on each of these cups.

Have your child count out 3 quarters each in two more cups. Write the numeral 3 on each of these cups.

Make a third pair of cups with 6 quarters in each cup and write the numeral 6 on each of these cups. Make a fourth pair with 10 in each cup and write 10 on each cup.

Have your child put on the blindfold and stretch her hands out, palms up. Set a cup with 1 quarter in one hand and ask your child to feel the weight of the cup.

Set a cup with 6 or 10 quarters in your child's other hand and ask, *"Do they weigh the same, or are they different?"* Your child should say that they feel different. Ask him which one feels *heavier* and which one feels *lighter* than the other.

Your child opens her eyes and checks to see that the cups have different numbers of coins and whether or not she identified the heavier / lighter cup correctly.

NOTE: If your child says that the cups feel like they weight the same, try letting her feel them with her eyes closed, but without the blindfold, so she gets familiar with how they feel. You can also make the difference in the numbers of coins greater to make the difference in their weights easier to feel. If these steps don't help, bring the activity to a positive conclusion. Look for opportunities to have your child feel everyday items to compare their weight. Try the activity again in a few weeks or months.

Extensions

Use **pennies and nickels**. See how many more coins you have to add for your child to be able to feel that one cup is heavier than the other. Test different members of your family to determine everyone's **weight sensation threshold**.

Gradually give your child cups with less difference in how many quarters each cup holds. See if your child can develop the ability to recognize a difference of as little as 1 quarter.

With a younger child, try this interesting experiment. Find a few objects that are **small but fairly heavy**, like a dense rock, a heavy piece of solid glass, or an exercise barbell. Now find objects that are **large but light**, such as a balloon, a large styrofoam figure, or a large, hollow piece of plastic fruit. Set one of each in front of your child and ask which one she thinks is heavier. Repeat with other combinations. Until a child develops enough ability to use abstract thought and reasoning, he will often think that any larger object must also be heavier.

"An adult if he is to provide proper guidance, must always be calm and act slowly so that the child who is watching him can clearly see his actions in all their particulars."

Maria Montessori

Thermic Touch

The Montessori Thermic Bottles (left) allow a child to grade bottles of water by **temperature**. They cost $40-65. At home, you can do the same activity with **8-10 unopened mini-bottles of water** (250ml plastic bottles).

Put two bottles in the freezer for 10 minutes or so (experiment). Put two more in your refrigerator for the same time period. Two more stay at room temperature. Another pair are heated in the microwave for 40 seconds or so (experiment). Get them all together and let your child feel them and make pairs by matching them based on their temperatures. Exercise good safety awareness with this activity to avoid skin damage with bottles that are either too hot or too cold – test all bottles yourself first.

Hearing

When you are out with your child, stop a moment and see what sounds you can identify. Birds chirping, construction equipment, shopping carts, people talking – help your child isolate out the different sounds around him. The following activities will then help your child develop auditory acuity and discrimination.

What Is That?

Search You Tube and Google for different sounds and save them on your phone or tablet. Play them for your child and take turns trying to figure out what they are. Examples:

door slamming	rain	car starting
children playing	clothes dryer	bouncing ball
dog barking	loud wind	alarm clock

crumpling paper	heartbeat	drum roll
breathing	footsteps	hammering nails
bees	locomotive	vacuum cleaner

There are many good **iPad apps** for focusing on sounds, including:

Animal Sounds	**Let's Hear The Animals!**
What's That Sound?	**Mini-Adventures Animals**
Zoola Animals	**Mini-Adventures Music**

Sound Matching

This activity can be done many ways. All involve making up pairs of containers, each pair filled about 1/3 full each with the same material. The child at left is using plastic easter eggs. Two have rice, two have salt, two have beans, two have coffee, etc. The eggs are *not* matched by color, as that would defeat the purpose of the activity, which is matching them based on their **sounds**. The eggs have been glued shut to prevent accidents. The child is shaking them next to her ear and making pairs by finding eggs that sound the same. *Tot School photo*

Other good containers for making sound pairs are Glad Mini-Round 4oz. food containers, old style camera film canisters, and identical empty spice bottles with labels removed. Make up at least 5-8 pairs each time using different materials. The advantage of easily opened containers is the ease with which you can try new materials. If your child is younger and has more trouble hearing the difference between sounds, use materials that are very different, like coins and salt. As your child's auditory acuity and discrimination improve, use materials with more subtle sound differences, such as flaked cereal and rice. Let your child come up with ideas and experiment. Try many different materials.

Identifying Tones

All this activity for 4-6 yr. olds requires is three identical drinking glasses, water with food coloring, a dinner knife, three strips of paper, and a dry erase marker. Leave one glass empty. Fill the second 1/2 full with water; and the third almost full with water. Help your child as needed to write **highest, middle**, and **lowest** on the strips of paper in lower case letters. Show your child how to strike the sides of the glasses with the knife and listen to the tone each one makes. Help your child identify the empty glass as the highest, the almost full glass as the lowest, and the 1/2 full glass as the middle tone.

Strike the empty glass and tell your child, "*This glass has the highest tone.*" Set the **'highest'** slip in front of the glass. Repeat with the other glasses, identifying the 1/2 full glass as the **'middle'**, and the almost full glass as the 'lowest'.

Have your child close her eyes or put on a blindfold. Hit the highest and lowest tone glasses and have your child practice identifying them. Now include the middle tone and let your child practice identifying all three. Be sure to switch roles and let your child hit the glasses while you name the three tones.

iPad apps like **Easy Xylophone** make it easy to help your child identify high, low, and middle tones. You can make up and play 1-3 note sequences for each other and try to match them. Identify them with the letters of the notes (E,F,G, etc.) and write down your sequences.

Where is That Sound?

Young children have yet to develop a clear sense of their **body position in space**. They need help to understand **position concepts** like *left, right, above, below, in front, to the side,* and *behind.*

Use a bell, two objects to hit together, or your voice as the sound. Use a **blindfold**. The only other thing you need is a quiet space.

Spend a few minutes standing facing the same direction as your child and showing her by pointing which directions *in front, to the sides*, and *behind* her body are. Have your child close his eyes or put on the blindfold. (The blindfold helps focus attention) Stand behind your child and make a sound.

Ask your child, without moving his body, to point to where the sound is coming from. Ask, "*Is the sound coming from in front of you or behind?*" Talk about his answer, helping as needed.

Repeat, making the sound in front of, and then on each side, of your child. Ask after each sound, "*Is the sound coming from in front, behind, or to the side?*" Make sure your child does not move her body, just point.

When your child is pretty familiar with these terms, introduce *left, right, above*, and *below*. You may want to **do just one at a time and practice**, as learning left and right can take time. Switch roles and let your child make the sound while you point and say which direction it is coming from.

This activity can be used in many daily situations. Ask your child to get something that is to her left or right, in front of or behind her. Talk about these directions when you are walking. Ask where a sound is coming from and in what direction an interesting sight is.

Taste

Science has identified up to seven types of taste. For this activity, we will use the four traditional tastes: **sweet, sour, salty**, and **bitter**. Print these names on card stock and cut them out.

Gather **lemon juice,** a piece of **candy or some sugar, salt**, a piece of **unsweetened chocolate**, and a **blindfold**. Have some water at hand for your child to swish between tastes. Dissolve a bit of salt in water for the salty taste. Some lemonade or other fruit juice makes a nice treat after the tasting is finished. This activity blends very nicely into a cooking experience.

Ask your child if he would like to see what a few different things taste like. Have your child set out a plastic mat and bring the cups, name cards, and things to taste to it.

Show your child the name cards and have him repeat the names. Have your child put on the blindfold. Start with the lemon, or lemon juice. Let your child put a little on his tongue and wait for the reaction! Explain that this kind of taste is called *sour*. Put the sour name card in front of that cup or the lemon. Let your child wash his mouth with a little water.

Now do the rest: potato chips or salt dissolved in water – *salty*; candy or plain sugar – *sweet*; and unsweetened chocolate – *bitter*. Let your child take a drink of water between each taste and put each name card with its taste. Read the name cards with your child. As you prepare foods and serve meals, talk about how things taste. Try to identify these tastes in different foods.

Smell

As with the other senses, taking time to be aware of and point out different smells in your child's environment is the first and easiest way to develop your child's **olfactory acuity and discrimination**. Food, flowers, plants, your pets, your bodies, a smoky fire; there are limitless opportunities. Don't avoid unpleasant smells - every sensory experience adds to your child's brain architecture. The kitchen is an obvious place to experience smells of all kinds. Young children have sensitive noses, let your child use hers!

What is it?

All you need are things with distinctive smells and a blindfold. Use easy to name objects, like cookies, fruits, a flower, green grass, clean laundry, a household cleaner (pledge, windex) sprayed on a cloth, a candle with a distinctive odor, flavors of Kool Aid, or spices that you help your child learn the names of, like cloves or cinnamon.

Have your child put on the blindfold and hold the items next to her nose so she can identify them. Practice and try different things. Switch roles and wear the blindfold while your child hands you things to smell and identify. You can make name cards for the items to add more language to the activity.

Can you Taste without Smell?

Cut similar, bite size slices of an apple and a potato. Have your child hold her nose closed tight and taste each slice. Could she tell the difference? Now let her taste more of each with her nose open. Why do they taste stronger and different? Smell and taste work together to help us enjoy our food. Try more foods this way.

Spice Smell Matching

This is like the Sound Matching activity on page 94, but using smells. Many Mom Blogs show some pretty fancy versions of this material. The simplest material of all uses **spices** poured into **clear condiment or plastic cups**. All you need is a **blindfold** and you are ready to go. This setup lets you change materials easily and experiment matching all kinds of smells with minimal fuss.

Use 8-10 cups to start to make up 4-5 pairs of spice cups. Good starter spices include Mrs. Dash, ground cinnamon, cumin seed, ground thyme, and vanilla bean. Dry ground coffee, scented bath salts or soap shavings, and cotton balls with a few drops of scent can also work.

As with the Sound Matching, have your child put on the blindfold. Hold a cup under her nose and let her smell. Hold the matching cup to her nose and let her smell that one. Ask, *"Do they smell the same or different?"* If she correctly states that they smell the same, lift the blindfold and let her see the two matching cups. Open cups make it easy to visually confirm a match or mismatch. Continue until all the cups are matched, trying to fool your child as you go with mismatching smells. Switch roles and let your child hold up cups for you to smell and match. Try many different materials whenever your child is into doing this activity. Talk about all the names of the materials.

More Sensorial Activities

Here are more ideas for Sensorial materials you can make at home:

Size grading with wrenches.

Counting Coconuts

Colorful crafts sticks with magnets glued on the ends are used to build shapes on an overturned metal cookie sheet

Laura Ingalls Wannabe

These materials show the possibilities for using simple items to create highly interesting and educational early learning materials.

Left: Print out a family photo, lay crafts sticks side by side and glue on the photo, then cut between the sticks to create a photo puzzle. *Photo: What Do You Do All Day?* **Middle**: A plastic Kleenex box is repurposed by filling it with fabric scraps with various textures. Even a toddler can pull these out and get valuable tactile experience. *Photo: Counting Coconuts.* **Right**: A homemade lava lamp. Cooking oil colored with food coloring is mixed with water. Glue the lid on! *Photo: Chasing Cheerios.*

Left: Tactile Matching Balloons. Fill balloons with various materials with different textures, making 2 balloons with each material for your child to match.

Laura Ingalls Wannabe

Right: Red, Yellow, and blue food coloring mixed in a bowl of milk makes a color mixing activity. Your child can the secondary colors, even a rainbow!

Chasing Cheerios

Left: small glasses contain water with red, yellow, and blue food coloring. Paper towels are bridged between the glasses. The water wicks up and the colors mix. Cool!

Chasing Cheerios

Art & Music

Art projects promote free expression, muscle control and coordination, and explorations with color and line forms. Music resonates strongly with children. Music encourages movement and helps children absorb patterns and rhythms that promote intellectual growth.

The first two easy steps are to play good music in your home and make art materials available. Classical music, jazz, excellent vocals, and other high quality music provides all kinds of brain inputs. Fun kids' music encourages dancing and singing along. Children absorb the language in songs very easily. Play quality music and fun songs your child likes in the background in your home.

Art does not have to involve complicated, messy projects. Keeping art materials on hand allows your child to create something anytime. Colored pencils, crayons, and markers; sketch pads, colored construction paper, scissors, glue sticks, tissue paper, collage materials, pipe cleaners, watercolors, and tempura paints cover the basics. If you have room for and can afford a painting easel, these are great.

Collage

A sheet of construction paper or a paper plate creates the backdrop for endless collage creations. White glue, a glue stick, and various materials allow a child to glue up all kinds of artwork. Good collage materials include tissue paper scraps, beans, rice, corn, beads, pasta shapes, glitter, stickers, yarn pieces, fabric scraps, cotton balls, foil, straws, and cut up newspapers and magazines. There are many more. Encourage your child to combine drawing, painting, and collage elements.

Blogs for Art Projects

Many excellent Mom Blogs describe more art projects than your child could ever do. Check out these blogs for starters:

The Crafty Crow	Pink and Green Mama
Chasing Cheerios	Tot School

No Time For Flash Cards

The Activity Mom

Toddler Approved

The Home Teacher

Chocolate Muffin Tree

What Do You Do All Day?

Fine art prints hung in your home allow your child to absorb excellent examples of high quality art. Inexpensive fine art posters are available at **AllPosters.com**. Find inexpensive frames at **Displays2go.com**.

There are many great **iPad drawing and artwork apps**. Some make excellent use of the digital art capabilities of tablet devices. Here are a few:

Blackboard To Write

Dibu's Monster Maker

Splash of Color

Forge of Neon

Uzu

Kaleidescope Drawing Pad

Imagics+

Let's Create! Pottery

Drawing Pad

Faces iMake

Wow Doodle

Flowpaper

Artonics

PicsArt Kaleidescope

Flowscope

Tripping Fest Drawing

Melissa & Doug's Band In A Box is a nice collection of simple musical rhythm instruments that will let your child explore creating beats and producing different sounds.

The **Mini Chimalong** is a classic music toy that has won numerous awards. Children love it, it is well made, and it teaches the musical scale. Your child can play songs right away with the color coded guide.

 A simple xylophone is a great early musical instrument for children. It can be used for both percussion and playing melodies. Amazon has them for $15-40. The **Hohner Kids Toddler Glockenspiel** (different kind pictured) gets high ratings for sound quality and tone accuracy. You can write the notes on the bars with a marker.

Have your child turn away while you play a note. Play another note and ask your child if the notes sounded the **same or different**. Mix up the notes as you play, then let your child hit the notes while you turn away and answer '*same*' or '*different*'.

Teach your child the difference between **low and high** notes. Once she can distinguish and identify notes that are higher and lower, have her **try to hum along at the same pitch** as different notes. Strike the note on the xylophone repeatedly as your child adjusts his humming to match the note's pitch.

There are many excellent **iPad music apps** for kids, including:

iXylophone	**Kids Music Maker**
Magical Music Box	**The Day The Music Stopped**
Loopy Tunes	**Toddler Jukebox**
Songs 4 Kids	**My First Songs**

Good online sources of musical experiences for children include:

PBS Kids	**Free Kids Music**
Creating Music	**funschool.kaboose.com**
KiDiddles	**Childrensmusic.org**
Childrens Music on Sesame Street	**Kidsknowit**

"The things he sees are not just remembered; they form a part of his soul."

Maria Montessori

Digital Life

Todays children grow up with technology. It is a natural part of their lives. Learning to operate in the digital world is as imperative for young children today as learning to walk and talk. Technology has evolved so rapidly, however, that little actual research has been done on how best to introduce technology to young children and what the real benefits and pitfalls are. Here are two points to keep in mind:

- From birth to around six, children are gathering up an amazing storehouse of sensory information about the **real world**. Too much screen time short circuits this essential process, leaving children with a lack of raw material to use in organizing their brain architecture. Until around 3-4, the majority of a child's experiences should come through handling actual objects, body movement, and interacting with other children and adults.

- As discussed on page 14, another primary developmental task of three to six year olds is making the **passage into abstract thought**. A two year old will usually be more into objects than images. By four, the same child relates more easily to images and design, and is entering his sentitive period for reading and writing. By five to six, the child can relate to many aspects of the world by using thought, like older children and adults; and is well into using spoken and printed words, which are highly abstract line drawings.

These observations suggest a path for introducing digital technology to young children. Until around 3, we should strictly limit digital screen time and be sure our child is getting most of her experience interacting with the real world. Starting around 3, when the passage into abstract thought takes off, we can *slowly* introduce high quality educational tablet apps. Over the next three years, as he completes the passage into abstract thought, the child can use tablet apps more often. This approach offers a mix of real world and digital experience, each delivered at the right time and in the right proportions.

Choosing a Tablet and Apps

When the time is right for introducing educational apps, a tablet is nearly the perfect choice for preschoolers. They are child sized, have touch screens, and are fascinating to kids. Good apps are abundant, cheap, and cover most areas of learning. At the present time, and possibly for the foreseeable future, Apple educational apps are far superior to Android offerings. The difference is so striking that I recommend only iPad apps. If you are getting a tablet for a preschooler, I recommend an **iPad Mini** or a **full size iPad** with **32 gb of memory** and a **Retina display**.

Not all educational apps are created equal. Many are poorly sequenced, have distracting, whiz-bang visual effects, and include too much empty praise, with voices constantly shouting, *"You're great, Sweet, Good Job!"* Children do not need this. Reliance on outer praise can become a habit that prevents children from following their own path. Children get true satisfaction from mastering skills and information. Great apps have a clean, uncluttered look that helps a child focus in on the essential information or task. Too many distracting elements interefere with concentration.

When an app has reading or math elements, it is important to be sure your child experiences a **proper sequence** of challenges. For example, some math apps mix simple counting of groups of objects with addition of larger numbers and other more complex skills. Math is learned as a logical sequence of skills, each building on those that came before. Presenting challenges a child cannot be ready for is counterproductive. Take a close look at the sequence of skills provided in the Math (p. 131) and Reading (p. 152) sections to become familiar with how things progress in these areas.

Suggested apps

Here are examples of excellent educational iPad apps and game apps:

Bugs and Bubbles	**Bugs and Numbers**
Bitsboard	**Scribble Press**
Teach Me Kindergarten	**Zoo Train**
Grandpa''s Workshop	**Batlleship for Kids**

Labyrinth	Draw With Aquares
Tangram Puzzles	Flow Free
Grid Drawing for Kids	Mini Train for Kids
Air Hockey	My Play Home
Toca Kitchen	Jelly Car 3
Pool Break	Where's My Head?
Amazing Alex	Cut the Rope
Family Golf 3D	Sprinkle Jr.
Awesome Eats	Snuggle Truck
Dr. Panda's Hospital	Road Trip Bingo HD
Chess Free HD	Where's My Water?
Classic Simon	PBS Kids Video

More app recommendations are found throughout this book. **Common Sense Media** is a great source for information and ratings on apps. Use apps like **App Shopper** and others to keep an eye out for free apps.

Videos

Videos are becoming a primary teaching tool for children. Well produced, visually rich videos can quickly teach complex concepts far more easily than hundreds of pages of dry text. Our children are becoming '*show me*' learners. **You Tube** has thousands of short, wonderful videos preschoolers can watch on just about any topic. **Lots to Learn** is You Tube's own collection of preschool early learning videos. **Turtle Diary** is a free site with all kinds of educational, animated videos. An **Apple Tv** or **Roku 3** set top box allows you to stream internet content to a large screen TV.

As your child grows, when he expresses an interest in something, search for child-appropriate videos about it and save them on your You Tube playlist or as bookmarks on your browser, organized into folders by topic. This allows your child to find her favorite videos herself and watch them multiple times. Repetition is essential for learning.

Protect your child's eyes and ears

Improper use of headphones can negatively impact your child's hearing. Even a short burst of loud sound through headphones can cause **immediate hearing loss** in children. Get your child **volume-limiting headphones** and make sure she uses them.

Science

Kids love science. A 4 year old has no tests or chapters to read, no arbitrary benchmarks to measure her learning. She explores the world like a true scientist, with a thirst for knowledge. To a young child, science is magic and secrets unfolding. Do these activities as your child's interests dictate, in a spirit of fun, exploration, and discovery.

"It is necessary to place the soul of the child in contact with creation, in order that he may lay up for himself treasure from the directly educating forces of living nature."

Maria Montessori

Can plants grow without soil?

 Sprouting beans is a great way for a child to experience how plants start their lives and grow. Let your child help with all the steps. Pinto, kidney, black, or Chinese green beans will all work. Gather some, and let your child pour them into a small bowl. Show how to wash and drain the beans, using one hand to keep them from falling out of the bowl. This adds a new challenge. Let your child cover the beans with plenty of water, enough so they won't soak it all up, and let them sit overnight.

In the morning, drain the water, cover the bowl with a clean cloth, and set it out of direct sunlight and direct heat. A high shelf inside a kitchen cabinet works well. Rinse the beans with water and drain 1-2 times a day for 2-3 days, keeping the beans in the same dark or semi-dark spot.

In a couple of days, you should see the beans sprouting. Let your child taste a few. The sprouts will continue to grow until they get pretty large. Pick a nice one and take a closer look. Using a magnifying glass works well. The seed pod itself is the **cotyledon**. Point out the **root**. It will probably have little hairs at the end to soak up water. The **primary leaves** are the first leaves on the stem, usually a pair. Let your child try **drawing a sprout**, and check out **videos of sprouts** growing on You Tube. To extend the activity, plant some sprouts in potting soil with the root and seed pods covered.

Get into gardening!

Gardening is one of the best possible science experiences for children. They can help prepare the soil, plant seeds, and water and care for their own flowers, vegetables, and beans. You can create a garden plot or just use pots on a patio.

Plants in pots can become self-contained Practical Life activities. Add a small spray bottle of water and cotton balls and your child can wash the leaves. Show her how to use her finger to see if plants are dry. Dead leaves can be pruned. The health of the leaves and stem can be checked.

Gardening is a fantastic opportunity for cooperative family projects. Shopping for supplies; preparing plots, pots, and soil; watering and caring for plants and flowers, learning about insects, making flower arrangements, eating vegetables - the opportunities for early learning are endless.

Check out Gardening with Children at **eartheasy.com**, and Gardening With Small Children at **reneesgarden.com**.

Some good **iPad plant apps** are: **Parts of Plants, Gazzili Science, Life Cycle, Seed Cycle**, and **Parts of a Plant**.

"We especially need imagination in science. It is not all mathematics, nor all logic, but it is somewhat beauty and poetry."

Maria Montessori

Sponge Salad

Buy a pack of Cress seeds and a new, rough textured sponge. Rinse the sponge several times with clean water and lay it in the dish. Sprinkle cress seeds over the top of the sponge. Add some water to the dish. In about a day the seeds will crack open. They will start to root in about three days, and probably by the next day will have leaves. When they get big enough, trim them off with scissors and eat. Sponge farming!

How do plants drink water?

For this fun activity, all you need are Celery stalks (some with leaves), cup, water, red or blue food coloring.

Let your child fill the cup half full with water and put in a few drops of food coloring. If your child is cutting safely, she can cut about 5 pieces of celery about 5 inches long. Make nice clean cuts. Leave a few with the leaves on. Have your child put the pieces in the cup. Set the cup out of the way and wait a few hours.

When you return, examine the stalks. Color dots should be visible around the edges of the ends. Wait another day. Now, the bottom ends will be colored. The top ends should clearly show little dots of color at the end of each **vascular bundle** extending up the outside of the **stalk** just under the skin. The leaves should be dotted with color. Point out the lines on the outside of the celery and show your child that they are tubes going up the stalk. Explain that the water traveled up the celery by **capillary action**. That is how plants get a drink.

To further demonstrate capillary action for your child, add food coloring to a little water in a dish. Have your child tear off a piece of paper towel and dip one end in the colored water. The water will travel up the towel. That is how water travels up the vascular bundles in the plant stem.

Growing carrot leaves

Cut about ½" off the top of a few carrots. Find a shallow dish and put ½" or so of sand in it. Add water until the sand is all wet but no water is visible on top. Push the carrot tops a little bit down into the sand. Let them sit in a well-lit area and don't move them. Add water if the sand dries out. In a couple of weeks, you should have leaves. They will continue to grow as long as you water them.

Plant printables

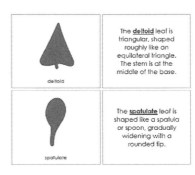

Montessori Print Shop has a superb collection of printable materials related to flora and fauna. Check out their science materials for ideas. These classroom quality materials help encourage your child's development of abstract thinking abilities. They are the perfect extension of your child's hands-on materials.

Make Transpiration bags

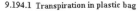

9.194.1 Transpiration in plastic bag

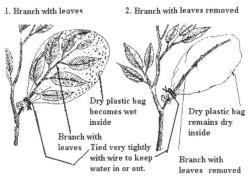

1. Branch with leaves

2. Branch with leaves removed

Dry plastic bag becomes wet inside

Branch with leaves

Tied very tightly with wire to keep water in or out.

Dry plastic bag remains dry inside

Branch with leaves removed

Transpiration is the loss of water, mostly through leaves. Find a branch with healthy leaves, and remove the leaves from a nearby branch. Tie a clear plastic bag *securely* over each with a zip tie. Wait two days and check. The bag over the leaves should have water in it. Why is the bag over the other branch dry? This ties in nicely with the previous activity showing how plants drink. Once the water travels up to the leaves, some of it returns to the atmosphere by transpiration.

Get up close

A **magnifying glass** opens up a new world of science discovery. Look at plants, insects, rocks, your skin, almost anything of interest. When your child is older, a microscope can extend these observations into the world of microorganisms, crystals, cells, and other amazing things!

Check out your habitat

Search habitats like wetlands, forest, desert, ocean, grasslands, and others on You Tube. What habitats exist where you live? In every habitat, living things need the same things to survive: **shelter, air, water, food**, and **space**. Identify these in habitats near you. Good **iPad habitat apps** include:

The Forest for iPad

Magic School Bus – Oceans

Ecosystems HD

Take an online safari

Search mammals, birds, insects, fish, crustaceans, amphibians, and reptiles with your browser and on You Tube. Check out the images and videos and save the ones your child really likes in each category. Let your child cut them out and paste them into a homemade book about animals. This activity teaches your child about gathering information online – an essential skill today – as well as about all kinds of animals. Good **iPad animal apps**:

Montessori Approach to Zoology – Parts of Animals	Find Them All – Looking For Animals
Preschool – Animals and Their Young	Animal Sounds – Fun Toddler Game
Franklin Frog	Parker Penguin
Montessori Animal Kingdom	Mini Adventures – Animals
The Strange and Wonderful World of Ants	Bats! Furry Fliers of the Night
Zoola Animals	Photo Touch – Farm Animals

Bagel Bird Feeder

Let half a bagel harden overnight. Tie enough string through the hole and leave enough to hang the bagel outside. Have your child spread peanut butter on the bagel, then dip it into bird seed and hang it up. Sit by the window. This is for the birds!

Mama nirvana photo

A strategically placed bird bath can be another wonderful way to observe birds doing their thing. If you are lucky, they may make a nest. Encourage this with a homemade birdhouse. Great kits are available at Lowes and Home Depot and online. This adds a super Practical Life activity. Let your child paint the birdhouse to bring art into it. Multi-step activities like this pack a big learning punch.

Make Fossils

Press plastic insects into a sheet of playdoh and separate them to make your own fossils. Bury these in a bowl of beans for your little archeologist to discover. You can press them into cookie dough to make fossil cookies.

The Education of Ours photo

Good **iPad dinosaur apps** include:

Scholastic First Discovery: Dinosaurs

Britannica Kids: Dinosaurs

The Magic School Bus: Dinosaurs

Journeys With Dinosaurs

Fossil by Claire Ewart

Fantastic Dinosaurs

Discover your body with the iPad

iPad apps for helping children learn about the parts of their bodies include:

Discover Your Body HD

Parts of the Body for Kids

This is My Body

Bitsboard

Search You Tube for the many excellent videos for children about the human body. There are videos on every body part and system.

These Bones of Mine

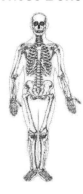

Search online and print a picture of a human skeleton. Title a sheet of paper 'Bones of mine that I can feel.' Have your child start with the fingertips of one of hand. She can squeeze her fingers one by one, feeling for the bones under the skin. Some bones are easier to feel – like the knuckles where bone sections join. Have your child bend a finger and feel each knuckle. Repeat with other joints like the wrists, elbows, shoulders, hips, knees, and ankles. Feel these parts of your own body as well.

Bones of mine that I can feel	
fingers	chin
knuckles	sternum
hand	ribs
wrist	hip
forearm	knee
elbow	ankle
shoulder	foot
jaw	toes
head	spine

Write the names on the sheet and draw an arrow to the bones he finds. Help your child as needed to find her fingers, knuckle, wrist, forearm, upper arm, shoulder, chin, jaw, head, sternum, ribs, spine, hip, knee, ankle, foot, and toes. Do the same bones on each side feel the same?

Have your child feel for bones down one side of her body and then the other. Include the same spots on each arm and leg, as well as the skull, jaw, sternum, and ribs. If your child is writing now, have him write down a list of all the bones he can feel on the sheet of paper. Do this for her if she is not quite ready yet. Save this sheet and use the words as practice sight words when your child gets to that point in the Reading Sequence.

A great set of **25 Skeleton Three Part Cards** is available from **Montessori Print Shop**. See page 38 for directions on using these.

Save a leg and thigh bone from a chicken dinner. Clean them well and let your child examine them. Feel how strong they are and how hard to bend, even though they are very light. Get a large, raw, marrow bone at the market and examine the center. The middle is filled with **bone marrow.** This where our **blood cells** are made. Get some of the marrow out with a fork or toothpick, spread it thin, and examine it with a magnifying glass.

To make an **artificial joint**, tape the ends of two paper towel rolls together by bridging the tape between them. Now the rolls move back and forth like your knee or elbow joints. Can you find more joints?

Fun **iPad apps** about the skeleton include **Dem Dancing Bones**, and the excellent **D. Bones.**

Take Your Pulse

With your child, locate the radial artery pulse point. Move a little closer to the thumb if you can't quite feel it with two fingers pressing lightly at the point shown. Feel your heartbeats. Do they feel the same? Count yours or your child's pulse for 60 seconds, or do 30 seconds and double it, to find your **pulse rate**. The normal range for the resting pulse for an adult is 60-90 beats / minute, and 70-100 beats / minute for a child. If you have been exercising, your pulse rate will be higher. Count your pulse rates at rest, then do jumping jacks for a few minutes and count them again. Write down all the results and compare.

Listen to Your Heart

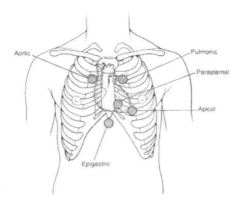

Buy an inexpensive stethoscope online or at a nurse's uniform shop. Bend the earpieces forward a little, insert them into your ears, and tap the face to be sure you are hearing through it properly. Make the room quiet and do not talk. Hold the face of the stethoscope at any of the points shown, placing it between ribs. The Pulmonic and Apical points usually work the best. Listen to your heartbeats. A normal heartbeat has a "*Lub-dub*" sound.

To illustrate how a heart beats, blow up a small balloon. Squeeze the top half and let go, then squeeze the bottom half and let go, and repeat, back and forth. That is how your heart beats. First the upper two chambers – the **Atria** – beat, and then the lower chambers – the **Ventricles** – beat. Search You Tube for the many good heartbeat videos suitable for children. There are more that show the entire **Circulatory System**.

Feel your lungs

Have your child hold the sides of her chest as she takes a big breath and then exhales, while feeling her hands move out and in as she breathes in and out. Our lungs are like two balloons in our chest that expand and contract as we breathe. Use a bunch of grapes to show your child what the air sacs, or alveoli, in our lungs look like. Ours are much smaller, though!

Listen to your breathing

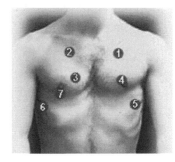

Use your stethoscope to hear your lungs breathing. In a quiet room, place the stethoscope at the points on the chest shown and breathe deeply, through your mouth. You should hear air swooshing in and out of your lungs.

Reocities.com photo

Listen to your gastrointestinal tract

Using your stethoscope, listen to your belly in many places above, below, and to each side of your belly button. You should hear gurgles, bubbling, pops, and other odd noises. These are all signs that your gastrointestinal tract is doing its thing, moving food through your body. These sounds will usually be louder after you eat. The natural waves of muscle movement that propel food through the GI tract are called **peristalsis**.

Let your child squish and mix saltine crackers or cereal with water and food coloring in a closed zip lock bag to show how food mixes in the **stomach**. Now, let him squish cooked instant oatmeal through a panty hose leg with the end cut off, or a balloon, to see how food travels down the **intestines**.

There are many wonderful You Tube videos and images online to show your child how the GI tract looks and works, and all of its parts.

How far can you feel?

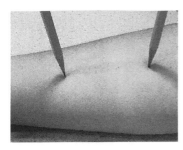

Sensor cells under our skin called **Meissner's Corpuscles** react to light pressure and touch. There are more of them in some places than others on our bodies. To find out where these places are, do the **Two Point Touch** experiment. Sharpen two pencils. Have your child put on a blindfold and hold out his arm. On the inner side of the forearm, press the two pencils down with their points very close together, within ¼" of each other. Ask your child how many pencils he feels. He should say one. Now, move one pencil away from the other about ¼", press them both down, and ask again. Continue until your child says that she feels two points. Let her remove the blindfold and repeat the experiment so she can see what is happening. Repeat the experiment on different parts of the body. Where the distance is the greatest between the points when your child can feel two points, there are the *fewest* Meissner's Corpuscles. See if you can find out which areas of the body have more than others.

Does smell affect taste?

Carefully using a food grater, let your child help you grate up some **apple, potato, carrot,** and **onion**. Have your child put on a blindfold. Let him taste the apple, then some potato. Now, hold her nose closed firmly and try it again. Do they taste different this time or is it hard to tell which is which? Try the other foods and compare to see if they taste differently with the nose closed.

Our sense of smell is intimately tied into our sense of taste. Odor molecules enter our nose as we place food on our mouths, helping our brain identify different foods.

My Amazing Hands

This great activity uses your child's hand to introduce types of **measurement**. All you need is a **bowl of water** filled to the brim and deep enough to submerge your child's fist, a **larger bowl** to set that one inside, **kidney beans**, a sheet of **graph paper**, a **measuring cup** with a ml scale, a **tape measure**, and a **pencil or marker.** Have your child bring it all to a table.

Have your child trace his hand on the paper. Help only if needed to get a pretty accurate tracing. Use the tape measure and measure from the wrist to the tip of the longest finger. Show your child the reading on the tape. Write down: **Length = _____ inches.**

Help your child count how many squares on the graph paper lie within the tracing outline. Count partially covered squares as one square. Write down: **Surface Area = _____ squares.**

Have your child grab a handful of beans, and then empty her hand in an empty dry bowl. Count the beans. Write down: **Capacity = _____ beans.**

Set the bowl with water filled to the brim inside the other bowl. Have your child make a fist and push it all the way into the bowl with water. Water will spill out into the outside bowl. Carefully remove the inside bowl and let your child dry his hand. Have your child pour the water in the larger bowl into the measuring cup. Help as needed to read how many ml of water are in the cup. Write down: **Volume = _____ milliliters of water.**

Classification: Sink & Float

This experiment in the buoyancy of objects is a preschool favorite. Have your child fill a pretty deep bowl about 2/3 full with water. Make two signs that say **Sink**, and **Float**. Gather some objects to test in another bowl and get a towel.

Good test objects include a clothespin, paper clip, coin, rubber band, marker, poker chip, plastic toys, bolt, pencil, small rubber ball, and a pine cone. Many objects will work, just get a variety that will fit in the bowl. Have your child place the bowl in the center top, with the signs on either side, and all the objects in the middle.

Select an object and ask, *"Do you think this will sink to the bottom, or float on the top of the water?"* Get your child's response, then let her place the object in the water and see. Have your child dry it and place it under the correct sign. Repeat until all the objects are sorted.

Extensions

Next, do the same experiment, but with a **horseshoe magnet** from a hobby store. Have your child try to pick up a variety of metal and non-metal objects with it to see if they are **Magnetic** or **Non-magnetic**.

Make up signs that say **Curved-sided**, and **Straight-sided**, and classify another group of objects (including the **Geometric Solids**, p. 83) based on this characteristic.

Extend the activity into images with pictures downloaded from the internet of objects and animals that are found on **Land**, in the **Air**, and in **Water** (p. 78). Other classification activities:

Plant and Animal

Fish, Bird, Mammal, Reptile, Crustacean, Amphibian, Insect

Wood, Metal, Plastic, Glass, Ceramic, Fabric

Vertebrate or Invertebrate

Types of clouds

Salt & Sugar Magic

All you need for this is **salt, sugar, water**, and **two microwave-safe, clear cups**. Let your child fill the cups about ½ full with water. Have her spoon a little salt into one, and sugar into the other, and then stir each until both are all dissolved in their cups. Ask, *"Where did the salt and sugar go?"*

Explain that the salt and sugar dissolved in the water. Ask, *"Do you think we can ever get the salt and sugar back again?"*

Pour off all but a little of the water in each cup. Place them, one at a time, into the microwave and cook them until the water has boiled off. There should be salt and sugar clinging to the sides of each cup when you are through. They have reappeared!

Set some of the water from each cup aside on a sunny window ledge for a few days and let the water evaporate off for the same effect.

Baking soda & vinegar

The Activity Mom describes this fizzy chemistry experience:

"Sprinkle baking soda onto a plate. Use a medicine dropper to drop vinegar onto the baking soda. Watch the fizzy reaction. B thought this was so cool! He didn't ask me WHY it was happening which I'm happy about because I wasn't prepared to answer that. I think my go to response for something like that in the future will be "Great question! Where do you think we could look to find that answer?"

Baking soda is a **base**, and vinegar is **acidic**. When an acid and a base meet, there is a **chemical reaction**.

Condensation and Evaporation

The next time you take a shower, leave the exhaust fan off and let the mirror over the sink get foggy. Ask your child why she thinks the mirror got wet when all the water was in the shower behind a curtain or closed door. How did the water get on the mirror? Explain that the hot water became **steam**, or **water vapor**, and floated in the air until it hit the cool mirror and turned back into water. This is called **condensation**.

Now, get your hair dryer out, turn it on, and blow on the condensation on the mirror until it disappears. The heat turned the water back into vapor again! That is called **evaporation**.

To demonstrate **condensation** again, fill a glass with ice cubes and water, set it on the counter, and wait 20 minutes. There should be water on the outside of the glass. Where did that water come from? It was already in the air. When the air hit the cool sides of the glass, the water **condensed** back into water on the outside of the glass.

Solid, Liquid, Gas

Set an ice cube on a plate. Water as ice is a **solid**. It has its own **shape** and takes up **space**. It does not change shape in our hands. Get a small jar and fill it to the rim with beans or uncooked rice. Tell your child this shows how the **molecules** that make the ice are tightly packed together in the ice. Don't worry about explaining in detail, your child is just absorbing information.

Let the ice melt. Water as a **liquid** has **no shape of its own, but takes on the shape of its container**. Liquid spreads out flat on the plate. Pour the water (add if needed from the faucet) into a cup and show your child how the water now has the shape of the cup. Remove about half the beans or rice from the jar and shake it to show your child that in a liquid, the molecules are able to move about more because there is more space between them.

Boil the water on the stove until it is gone. Under close supervision, let your child pour a little water into a small pan. Keeping your child at a safe distance, boil the water until it is gone, watching the **steam** that rises. Tell your child the water is turning into a **gas**. A gas is **matter we cannot see and that spreads freely everywhere in the air**. Remove all the beans or rice pieces from the jar and point out that the jar is not really empty - it is still filled with the air we breathe, which is a gas.

What changed in each case to make the water change? The temperature.

A supercool experiment

 Get a few plastic bottles of Dasani® or another brand of **reverse osmosis filtered drinking water** and a plastic water bottle filled with plain tap water. Place all the bottles in the freezer for about 2 hours. Check and see if the tap water is frozen yet. You want to take the bottles out when the **tap water is frozen but the filtered water is not**. This usually takes 2 - 2 1/2 hours, depending on the temperature of your freezer. At this point, the filtered water will be **supercooled**, which means cooled past the normal freezing point for water of 32 degrees F. Without handling it too roughly, take a filtered water bottle out and show your child that it is still liquid.

Now, hold the filtered water bottle firmly straight up and slap it down on pretty hard on a countertop. If you did it right, **the water will all turn to ice in a few seconds!** If it doesn't, the water was not supercooled. Leave the other filtered water bottles in the freezer a bit longer and try again. Try this, too: pour supercooled water *slowly* onto an ice cube placed in a bowl.

Stab a potato!

 Your child may not believe what she is seeing when you do this experiment - until she tries it. Get a potato and a straw. Hold the straw by the sides and try to stick it into the potato. Show your child how the straw bends easily. Try to stab the potato with it and watch the straw bend harmlessly. Ask your child, "*I wonder if there is a way we could push the straw right into the potato?*"

Hold the straw with your thumb firmly over the end. Stab the straw quickly into the potato. How could it do that? Your finger kept the air inside the straw. When you brought the straw down, the air compressed inside the straw and made it much stronger - strong enough to stab a potato. Let your child give it a try. Be sure he keeps his thumb firmly over the end of the straw.

How many coins?

An excellent exercise in estimation and critical thinking. Stand a quarter on its edge by pressing it into a little dab of playdoh on a countertop. Ask your child, *"How many pennies do you think it will take to make a stack as high as the quarter?"* Stack a couple of pennies so your child can see what you mean.

When your child has guessed, stack that many pennies and see if the stack is as high as the quarter. It should take 12 pennies, which is probably more than your child guessed. Repeat the experiment using a penny and a nickel on end.

Good Vibrations

Make a classic **string telephone** (top) by connecting two Styrofoam cups with yarn. Punch a hole in the bottom of each cup, thread the yarn through each hole, and tie a paper clip on each end to keep the yarn from pulling out. Allow at least 15 feet of yarn between the cups. You and your child each hold a cup and walk apart until the yarn is tight. One of you talks into your cup, the other listens.

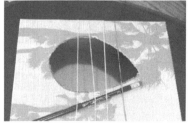

Make a **box harp** by cutting a hole in one side of a box (bottom), and stretching a few rubber bands around the box and over the hole. Use a pencil as shown as a bridge to lift the bands away from the box a bit. Your child can strum the harp with a finger or a dime and listen to the sounds. Try different thicknesses of rubber bands and bands of different sizes so some are really tight, others looser.

Your child should be able to see the rubber bands vibrating when they make sound. Check out the guitar strings at a music store next.

Electricity without wires

MyFunnyWorld.net

Static electricity is fun. You will need **balloons**, a **plastic comb, tissue paper**, a **wool sweater** (or your own hair), a **water faucet**, and an **aluminum can**.

Lay the can on its side. Rub an inflated balloon 20-30 times on your hair or a carpet. Hold the balloon a little ways from the can. The can should roll toward it.

Turn on the water faucet so it has the smallest stream of water that keeps its shape as a single stream. Comb your hair 20-30 times. Put the comb up close to the water at right angles to the stream and watch the water bend toward the comb.

Tear off a few very small pieces of tissue paper and lay them on the countertop. Comb your hair 20-30 times. Place the comb above the paper pieces and watch them jump up to the comb.

Rub an inflated balloon up and down against your hair, a wool sweater, or a carpet. Hold it a few inches from your hair. Did your hair stand out straight? Do it again and stick the balloon against a wall.

If you have carpet in your house, put on socks and walk while rubbing your feet against the carpet, then touch a metal doorknob. Did you get a spark?

Where in the world am I?

Take a trip with your child from your house to outer space. This activity is probably better for 5-6 yr. olds, but even younger children can have fun using **Google Earth**. Search Google Earth for the free download if you don't have it already – this wonderful resource belongs on every child's computer and iPad.

You should also download **Google Maps**, and get **paper maps** of your city, country, and the world, as well as a traditional globe. Using all these resources helps reinforce the information and concepts in multiple ways.

Start by walking to the end of your street and reading the **name of your street**. Have your child say it. Walk back to your house, and read the number on your house. Write down your **house number address and street name**. Have your child do it if she is writing now.

Find your street and the location of your house on Google maps, Google Earth, and your paper city map. Add the **name of your city** under your house address you wrote above.

Zoom out to your state map, open the paper country map, and find your state. Have your child mark it on the map and say your state's name. Add your **state name** to the sheet under the city name.

Zoom out on Google Earth to show your country, and look at the globe if you have one, and find your country on it. Have your child say your country name and add the name to your sheet.

Zoom out to show the entire planet. Add '**Planet Earth**' to your sheet.

On Google Earth, type in your address, hit enter, and 'fly' to your house. Then gradually zoom out again to see your city, state, the U.S., and our earth from space. You can add '**Our Solar System**' to the sheet.

Exploring Google Earth

Google Earth can occupy many hours of exploration. Explore everything this wonderful program has to offer. It is an amazing resource. Visit the **Google Earth Tutorials**.

Find and name the continents, oceans, and the world's great rivers.

Travel to the world's great cities. Zoom in on cities around the world and see how people live in Egypt, China, South America, anywhere.

Use *Panoramio* and check out the many photos from all over the world.

Use *Street View* and tour more than streets, cities, and neighborhoods. You can also discover natural wonders, Antarctica, the Grand Canyon, and the Swiss Alps!

Explore the great mountain ranges, rain forests, oceans, deserts, and mountains. *Earth View* is also available in Google Maps

Look at the topography of the earth under the oceans.

Use *Google Earth Sky*, visit galaxies, and see amazing astronomical sights.

Learn the continents and oceans

Recommended iPad geography apps include: **National Geographic World Atlas, iLearn Continents, iWorld Geography: Continents, Montessori Approach To Geography**, and **Globe for iPad**.

Montessori Print Shop has excellent continent printables, such as the **Continent Three Part Cards** (left). Their **World Flash Cards** are also good. Find many more at this wonderful online supplier.

To learn about **land and water forms**, Google terms like these and others you think of, and check the images and videos links:

lake	bay	isthmus
peninsula	strait	island
river	delta	mountain
valley	volcano	canyon
desert	archipelago	plain
plateau	cliff	swamp
cave	pond	marsh
waterfall	mesa	glacier

If you have any of these near where you live, be sure to visit. The iPad app, **Montessori Approach to Geography – Land & Water Forms**, is a good introduction.

"The child is both a hope and a promise for mankind."

Maria Montessori

Make a Volcano

Homeschoolblogger.com

Make a volcano with a baking soda & vinegar 'eruption'. First, do your child a big favor and visit **kids.discovery.com**. This site has wonderful interactive videos of volcanoes. You can even build your own virtual volcano.

Get a deep tray or tub. Find a small bottle, like an empty juice bottle, put it in the middle of a piece of cardboard, and build up a nice Play Doh volcano cone around it. Make the top of the cone even with the top of the bottle. Put the cap on until the cone is built. Your child may want to surround the cone with blue playdoh 'water' to make it a volcanic island; and perhaps add orange or red 'lava' coming down the sides.

Use a funnel if needed to put about a tbsp. of baking soda, a few drops of red food coloring, a tbsp. of dishwashing liquid, and a tbsp. of water into the bottle. Get the video camera ready. Get some newspaper and take the volcano outside for the eruption. Pour about a tbsp. of vinegar into the bottle and watch the volcano erupt.

Measure the Rain

Make a simple **rain gauge** using a sturdy glass jar that won't tip over in the wind. Let your child help hold a ruler against the side of the jar, and mark it at 1/2" increments with a black permanent marker. Set the jar outside when it starts to rain and see how much rain has fallen when it stops. Record the amounts on your child's wall calendar.

The Weather Channel is a good iPad app. Look at the forecast and radar maps of clouds moving with your child. See if the forecasted weather happens. **Quakefeed, Hurricane Tracker, Kid Weather**, and **Gazzili Science** are more good weather and geographic apps.

Solar System apps

There are many excellent iPad apps about our solar system and outer space, such as: **Montessori: Planets of the Solar System HD, Interactive Minds: Solar System, Solar Walk: 3D Solar System Model,** and **Planisphere**.

Why is the Moon Changing?

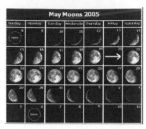

Watching the phases of the moon is a great science experience. **Moonconnection.com** has a **moon phase calendar** for every month of the year. Check to see if the moon looks like what the calendar says it will each night. When your child is ready, you can explain why the moon changes. This activity also gives a child practice with using the internet, a calendar, counting, and many new words.

Print out a moon phase calendar for the current month from the web site above. Go out tonight and take a look at the moon. Does it look like the calendar says it should on today's date? Match how the moon looks with the moon phase on the calendar that looks closest to it. Continue following the phases of the moon at night this way. If you miss a night or two, no worries, the moon changes rather slowly! You could schedule your moon observations on your child's calendar in her room (p. 148).

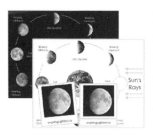

Montessori Print Shop has a nice **Moon Phase Chart** printable for your child's bedroom wall (left). **MoonPhase** is an excellent iPad app with all kinds of moon information.

Montessori Print Shop image

With a simple pair of binoculars, your child can examine the moon's surface. How did all those craters get there? Is there air around the moon? Why does the moon seem to be shining?

Mathematics

Children usually develop an increased interest in numbers in their third or fourth year. As your child uses Practical Life and Sensorial materials, there are many opportunities to count groups of objects like beans, blocks, straws, etc. At first, focus on identifying **groups of up to 10 identical objects** by counting them. Plenty of practice counting 1-10 objects is the foundation for math. With these experiences as background, it is easy to teach a young child about Math by using a logical sequence of activities.   *Photo: Julie Josey*

Encourage accurate counting

When your child counts, encourage her to slow down and **say each number exactly when her finger touches each object**. **1:1 Association** is a critical math concept. Children often get their counting and touching of the objects out of synch. Having your child point to objects with a pencil can work well.

Develop the foundation

Memorizing and repeating the numbers one to ten or higher does not mean your child understands math. Memorization of numbers, the alphabet, or almost anything else does not indicate true understanding. Math skills build gradually. The most important step is the first one, when a young child learns how to **group and accurately count and identify from 1-10 objects**. Spending time giving your child enough practice at each step on the math sequence will insure that he truly understands numbers. This will provide a firm foundation for success with math throughout the school years.

Tablet apps and worksheets

A child's first math experiences should be with **three dimensional objects**. There are excellent tablet math apps and worksheets, but parents should not be too quick to use them at first. Apps and worksheets are abstract representations. A young child needs a firm footing of experience with real objects before dealing with more abstract math work.

The exception to this is when you are starting with a 5-6 year old who already has some genuine math understanding and skills. After enough work with objects to be sure all the bases are covered, these children can work more with apps and worksheets.

Follow the sequence

The sequence of math activities and materials shown here are designed to be followed one after another, each building on the previous activities. The best way to insure that your child is successful is to follow the sequence.

Amounts 1, 2, and 3

 Gather **6 identical objects** – quarters, buttons (exact same size, shape, and color), identical poker chips, etc. Review how to do a **Three Step Lesson** (p. 35). Do a Three Step Lesson with groups of 1, 2, and 3 objects. Here is a guide:

Identify

Set one quarter down, touch it with your finger, and say, "*One. This is one.*" Have your child to this. Remove the quarter. Set down two quarters & repeat. Remove them, set down three quarters, & repeat.

Recognize

Set down **all three groups** of 1, 2, and 3 quarters. Ask, "*Can you point to where there are two?*" Repeat, asking your child to point out 1 and 3 quarters. Have your child close his eyes and switch the positions of the groups. Have him open his eyes and repeat. Play this game a few times.

Remember

Set down two quarters and ask, "*How many are there?*" Encourage your child to count. Remove the quarters and repeat with one and three quarters.

If your child cannot remember in step three, start over in step one and play more games in step two. Or, try it again in a few weeks after more counting practice.

Amounts 4, 5, and 6

Repeat **Three Step Lessons** with amounts of 4, 5, and 6 objects. Give your child plenty of time to practice counting and make sure she can identify these amounts correctly consistently. This is how you build a foundation for math. Remember to do 1, 2, and 3 also as a review.

Amounts 7, 8, and 9

Do **Three Step Lessons** with these amounts. Also review amounts 1-6.

Ten

Ten is the basis of our number system, so spend some extra time on it. Have your child count a number of different groups of 10 objects. Make a card with the numeral 10 on it and place it next to the groups of ten.

The next activities with numerals can actually be started when your child is doing amounts 7, 8, and 9.

Numerals 1, 2, and 3

Now you will need a set of **Montessori Sandpaper Numerals**. Check suppliers like Montessori Outlet online. They cost about $8. When your child looks at, says the numeral name, and traces the numeral with her first two fingers, she gets visual, auditory, and tactile input, which really helps get the information into her brain. These numerals, and the **Montessori Sandpaper Letters** (p. 153), have been used for over a hundred years with great results.

Do **Three Step Lessons** with the 1, 2, and 3 numerals. Each time your child first uses or identifies a numeral, have him **trace it with the first two fingers while looking at it and saying the number out loud.**

Numerals 4, 5, and 6

Do Three Step Lessons with these numerals until your child knows them well.

Numerals 7, 8, 9, and 10

Do Three Step Lessons until your child knows these numerals well.

Matching Amounts and Numerals 0-10

Now your work comes full circle as your child matches up the amounts and numerals she has learned. This will be the pattern all the way to 100: **learn amounts – learn numerals – match amounts and numerals**.

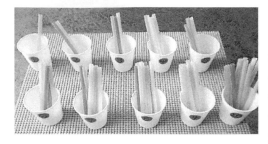

Get **11 identical plastic cups** and a **pack of straws**. Cut the straws in half. Write the numerals 0-10 on the cups, one numeral per cup. Have your child lay the cups out, starting on the left with zero and going left to right. Make two rows if needed. Let your child put the amount of straws in each cup that matches the numeral on each cup. Encourage careful counting. Point out that zero means nothing, or none, so it is left empty. Check your child's work by counting the straw groups with him. You can also put a rubber band around each group to illustrate groups as separate objects in themselves.

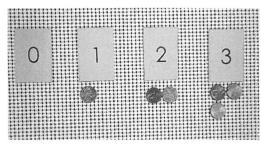

The next way to match amounts and numerals 0-10 is with **Cards & Counters**. Write or print up a set of numeral cards with the numerals 0-10 on them. Have your child lay the numerals out in order, left to right. Now he can place the correct number of pennies under each card. **Even numbers** will have matched pairs, **odd numbers** will have a penny without a partner at the end. This makes it easy to teach the concept of even and odd at a later time. Have your child match up all the way to 10, either laying out one long row of cards or making two rows, one above the other, if space requires.

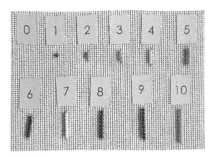

The final activity uses the **Montessori Teen Bead Bar Box**. This box of beads on wire costs around $8 at Montessori Outlet online. You will need these for activities to come, so get them now. Have your child match up the cards you made earlier with the correct bead bars.

Get free Cards and counters templates at **Montessori Print Shop**.

By the time most children get to this point, they can use **iPad math apps**. Good first apps include:

Intro to Math	Montessori Numberland HD
Montessori Numbers	Splash Money
Count 123	Learn to Count Numbers
Bugs and Numbers	Dominos Easy Match

Coin Exchange

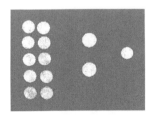

Gather **10 pennies, two nickels**, and a **dime**. Have your child count the pennies. Show her that 5 pennies = 1 nickel, 10 pennies = 1 dime, and 2 nickels = 1 dime. Go back and forth exchanging the coins. Practice all the possible combinations.

Amounts & Numerals 11-100

For the next activities you need the **Montessori Teen Bead Bar Box** (left), a box of **45 Golden Bead Ten Bars** (middle), and a **Hundred Golden Bead Chain** (right). These are inexpensive and very necessary tools.

All three will cost you around $25 total at **Montessori Outlet** and other online suppliers. A single disposable plastic toy that teaches your child nothing often costs more than this. These materials will give your child math skills for life, so they are a bargain. Sell them later to another parent and get half or more of your money back.

When you are sure that your child has fully mastered amounts and numerals 0-10, you can move on to **11-20**. After these are mastered, do **21-30, 31-40**, etc. all the way to **100**, using the activities shown next.

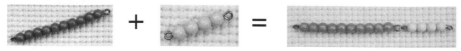

Using the **Montessori Teen Bead Bars** above, a **10 bar** (left) **plus a 4 bar** (middle) **equals 14** (right. This is how you will introduce, and your child will be counting, amounts from 11-100. Have your child use a sharpened pencil or similar object as a **pointer** when counting the beads. Make sure her pointing and counting stay in synch.

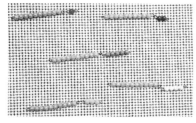

Now, do **Three Step Lessons** (p. 35), using the beads, with the amounts **11, 12**, and **13**. If your child is counting well, you can include **14** and **15**. At left is how a layout with all these looks in the second step when you are asking your child to recognize the amounts. Encourage your child to count to identify the amounts correctly. This reinforces the basic math you are working on.

Remember that in the first and last steps of a Three Step Lesson, only one of whatever you are teaching is shown. In the second step (shown above with amounts 11-15) you lay out all of them and ask your child to point out specific objects. Review the Three Step Lesson on p. 35 as needed.

When your child knows amounts **11-15** well, repeat **Three Step Lessons** with amounts **16-19**. When your child knows the **amounts 11-19** well, teach him the **numerals 11-19,** using printed cards. This is more effective with young children than using tablet apps. Handling the amounts and numerals is an important part of the experience. Here's how:

Print out or make numeral cards by hand. Make a bunch that say **10**, and another set exactly half that size with the numerals **0 – 9**. The photos above show how to teach your child the numeral **11**. Lay out the 10 and 1 cards as shown. Now, put the 1 card over the zero on the 10 card as you say, *"Ten and one say eleven."* Be sure you say '**say**' eleven rather than '**make**' eleven. You are not making amounts. When finished, your cards will look like those at right above, the numeral **11**.

Do **Three Step Lessons** with the numerals **11, 12**, and **13**. When your child has mastered these, do the numerals **14, 15**, and **16**. Finally do the numerals **17, 18,** and **19**.

Matching amounts and numerals 11-20

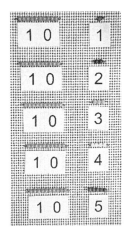
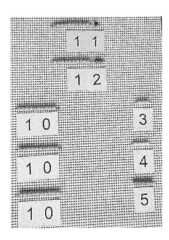

Lay out the Teen Bead Bars and numeral cards as shown. Make the **amount 11** by putting the ten and one bars together as you say, *"Ten and one makes eleven."* Make the numeral by putting the 10 and 1 cards together under the bars as you say, *"Ten and one says eleven."* Repeat with **12**. Let your child try making the rest. Help only as needed.

Make up a 20 numeral card and let your child count two ten bars and patch them with it. Repeat using 20 pennies. As with 10, **spend extra time on 20** to visually reinforce twenty as an amount and a numeral.

Amounts and numerals 21-100

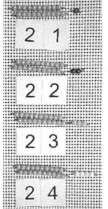

Repeat the sequence used for **11-20** with **21-30**, making more numeral cards as needed. Use two golden bead 10 bars to make twenty for each amount. At left is a layout showing amounts and numerals **21-24** after matching. As your child moves through the numbers toward 100, you may find that she catches on to the fact that each group of ten repeats (31, 32, 33; 51, 52, 53, etc.). This may make it possible for him to proceed more rapidly as he gets higher into the amounts and numerals. Encourage your child to **count by tens**, so that the beads do not have to be counted individually each time. Make sure she really understands and has counted them all first, however. **Montessori Print Shop** has a nice set of **Teen Beads, Boards, and Worksheets** printables for doing these activities. Good **iPad apps** for these activities include **Bitsboard** and **Pocket Chart Pro**.

Reinforcing and practicing

As you move through every set of 10 – the twenties, thirties, forties, etc., review and practice the amounts and numerals your child worked on before. Repetition and practice are essential to mastery. There are some additional activities you can do to keep things fresh and illustrate number concepts in new ways. The **Montessori Hundred Golden Bead Chain**, around $5 at Montessori Outlet, is an excellent, inexpensive materials for this.

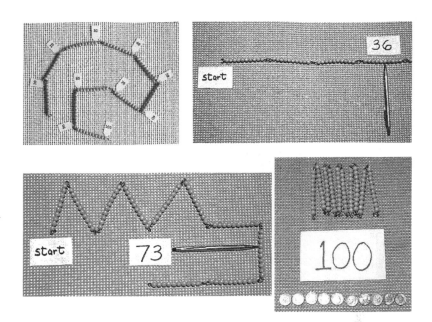

Top left: Make up a set of little pointer cards that say **10, 20, 30**, etc., up to **100**. Your child counts the chain and lays out the cards pointing at the proper beads as she counts up to 100. **Top right**: Write a number from 1-100 on a card. Your child lays out the Hundred Chain, and uses a pointer to count up to that number. Leave the pointer pointing at that bead. Your child reads the numeral card and sets it above the pointer. **Bottom left**: A similar activity, except that every set of tens is turned a different way as your child counts. This reinforces the concept of tens. **Bottom right**: Make up a 100 card. Reinforce that one dime = 10 pennies, so a dime can be used to represent 10. Lay out the Hundred Chain and 10 dimes with the 100 card to reinforce these concepts.

Make random numerals from 11-100 with the cards you have been using, and have your child make that amount using the beads. Switch roles and have your child both create numerals and create amounts for you to match. Do many different amounts and numerals to reinforce these essential math skills.

The Hundred Board

A **Montessori Hundred Board** is a well-made board with a blue base and a grid of lines, edged by a wooden frame that is raised on the sides to hold square 1-100 wooden numeral tiles. The numeral tiles come in a nice box.

The Hundred Board costs under $30 at Montessori Outlet and is a great investment in your child's math work if you can afford it. **Montessori Print Shop** offers the **1-100 Math Series**, a full set of printables that includes a Hundred Board, charts, numeral cards, and lessons, for only $3. Either will allow your child to experience the many math concepts illustrated by this versatile material. Good **Hundred Board iPad apps** include: **Hundred Board, 100's Board, Skip Counting,** and **Montessori Bead Skip Counting.**

Hundred Board activities

Have your child lay out 100 pennies on the board, starting at the top left corner and going left to right across each row working down, counting as she goes, from 1-100.

Now your child can lay out the numeral tiles or printed cards in the same way, 1-100.

Let your child count by tens and put a dime at the end of each row, or lay a golden bead ten bar at the end of each row. When finished, your child can skip count by tens from 10-100.

Have your child count the Hundred Board again, placing a nickel on every 5th square (5, 10, 15, 20, etc.), and then skip count by fives from 5-100.

Repeat the above activity, but placing a quarter every time your child reaches a multiple of 25. You can point out that 25 is two rows of squares on the board plus 5 in the next row down. Now, have your child skip count to 100 by 25's. This may take some recounting and practice. It will help to replace the quarters on the board with the numeral cards 25, 50, 75, and 100 before skip counting.

Extend your Hundred Board activities to using **money**. Show your child that 100 pennies, 10 dimes, and 20 nickels all = $1, using the Hundred Board.

Give your child numeral tiles or cards at random and let her find the correct place on the board for each by counting.

Fill the board with numeral tiles, then remove about 10-15 of the tiles at random. Let your child figure out which tiles are needed to fill the spaces and place those numerals on the board.

Explore **creating shapes** on the board using pennies. You can make a square, rectangles, arrows, stars, triangles, etc. See how many different shapes you can make and talk about their names.

Exploring larger numbers and the Decimal System

The **Hundred Board 101-200 iPad app** can help your child move into larger numbers.

Good iPad apps to use to teach your child the decimal system include: **Montessori Place Value, and Stamp Game.**

Montessori Print Shop offers a free **Printable Stamp Game and Instructions.**

Operations with Numbers

Now that your child has a good understanding of amounts and numerals 0-100, it is time to learn interesting things that can be done with them, like adding, subtracting, multiplying, and dividing. These can all be taught to 4-6 year olds with simple materials and a perhaps few iPad apps.

As your child learns to perform these number operations, look for real life opportunities for him to use these skills, such as in cooking when adding ingredients, determining how many of something to buy, dividing things up between people, etc.

Addition

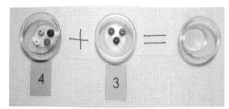

The easiest way to begin doing addition is with clear condiment or other small cups, wooden beads or similar objects, numeral cards, and cards that say + and =. Set them up as shown. Have your child empty the beads into the final cup and say, *"Four plus three."* Now, have her count the total and say, *"Four plus three equals seven."* Work on this with many amounts and numerals, sticking mainly to smaller totals for now, depending on where your child is at in learning amounts and numerals up to 100.

2 + 5 =	___	
3 + 6 =	___	
7 + 1 =	___	
5 + 4 =	___	
9 + 1 =	___	
4 + 3 =	___	
2 + 2 =	___	
5 + 3 =	___	
4 + 4 =	___	

Make a sheet of addition problems and have your child find the answers and write them down. Allow time for repetition and practice. You can make sheets that follow a pattern, 1+2, 1+3, 1+4, etc., which shows relationships between numbers. **iPad apps** for practicing addition include **Bead Facts**, and **Adding Apples HD.** The beautiful **Addition Strip Boards, Charts, and Instructions** printables from Montessori Print Shop are also excellent tools for home use.

Multiplication

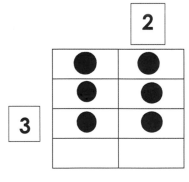

Use a blank Hundred Board printout or any grid of lines you print out or draw on paper. Make squares large enough to hold a penny. Tell your child, *"We are going to count to two, three times."* As you say this, lay a 2 card and a 3 card out as shown at left. Place two pennies in the top left squares, starting top left, and counting, "One, two." Do this again in the next two squares down. Repeat again in the next two squares down. "Now we counted to two, three times." Have your child count how many pennies are on the board.

On another sheet of paper or an index card, write out **2 X 3 = 6**. Say, *"Two times 3 equals six."* Make up many more problems and repeat these steps with each, listing all your multiplication problems on a sheet of paper.

1 x 0 = ___	2 x 0 = ___	3 x 0 = ___
1 x 1 = ___	2 x 1 = ___	3 x 1 = ___
1 x 2 = ___	2 x 2 = ___	3 x 2 = ___
1 x 3 = ___	2 x 3 = ___	3 x 3 = ___
1 x 4 = ___	2 x 4 = ___	3 x 4 = ___
1 x 5 = ___	2 x 5 = ___	3 x 5 = ___
1 x 6 = ___	2 x 6 = ___	3 x 6 = ___
1 x 7 = ___	2 x 7 = ___	3 x 7 = ___
1 x 8 = ___	2 x 8 = ___	3 x 8 = ___
1 x 9 = ___	2 x 9 = ___	3 x 9 = ___
1x10 = ___	2x10 = ___	3x10 = ___

When your child is familiar with the process, make up multiplication table sheets as above, all the way to the 10 X table. Have your child gradually do the problems and fill in the answers. This helps a child learn the relationships between numbers. Good **iPad multiplication apps** include **Multiplication HD** and **Skip Counting.**

Subtraction

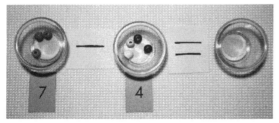

As with addition, start with real and similar objects, clear cups, and minus and equals signs. Set up a problem like the one at left and let your child put the right amount of objects in the leftmost cup. In this case, 7. Now read the problem, *"Seven minus four equals..."*. Have your child remove four from the 7 cup and put them in the 4 cup. Now your child pours the remaining objects in the first cup in the cup at the right side. Count them and put a 3 card under that cup. Read the entire problem. *"Seven minus four equals three."*

Make up many similar problems with all kinds of amounts as your child gets familiar with the process. Always encourage accurate counting.

Another easy way to illustrate subtraction is to thread 7 beads onto the left end of a string. Say, *"Let's take away three and see how many are left."* Let your child move three beads to the right end, counting to three as she does so, and counting the remaining beads at the left end. Say, *"Seven minus three equals four."* Do many similar problems.

Make up **subtraction cards,** like the multiplication cards shown on the preceding page, so your child sees the relationships between numbers.

Good **iPad** subtraction apps include **Subtracting Sardines**, and **Montessori Bead Facts Plus Minus**.

Montessori Print Shop offers excellent **Subtraction Strip Boards, Charts, and Instructions**.

Division

Be sure your child has practiced and has a firm understanding of addition, multiplication, and subtraction before attempting division. Division is a less intuitive operation, requiring a solid understanding of the other ways of manipulating amounts and numerals. These activities take your child into simple division with numbers that are equally divisible by other numbers, without remainders. You can certainly take it farther if your child has the interest, but these activities are great preparation for school.

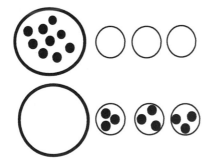

Have your child lay out a small bowl and three cups as shown at the top. Let her place 9 similar objects in the bowl. Now, she can place three cups next to the bowl, as shown. Say, *"Let's give three people each the same number of_____."*

Your child puts one object in each of the cups, counting 1, 2, 3 as he does this. Repeat twice more to divide up all the objects. Ask, "*How many* _____ *does each person get?*" Now, say, "*Nine divided into three groups, leaves 3 in each group*". Write out: **9 ÷ 3 = 3.** Do many similar problems.

The iPad app **Division Board** is excellent for division practice.

Good online math resources include:

Super Teacher Worksheets
Dad's Worksheets
Free Math Worksheets
Math Fact Cafe
PBS Parents Preschool & Kindergarten Math Games
Sheppard Software Free Math Games
Montessorimaterials.org
MontessoriMom.com

The Ordinal Value of Numbers

Ordinal value refers to the position or 'place' of an object in a sequence. The simplest way to do this is to line up a series of 10 objects. Say, "*We're going to count these a new way.*" Point to the first one on the left and say, moving your finger down the row, "*First, second, third, fourth, fifth,*" up to the tenth. Now let your child count the same way, helping her as needed if she forgets the terms.

Line up different objects and let your child practice counting them by their ordinal value. Test your child's understanding by asking him to point to the seventh, the second, the fifth, etc. The next time you are standing or parked in line somewhere with your child, ask her to figure out what place in the line you two are, helping as needed.

Look for other opportunities to introduce ordinal values, such as lining up food items when cooking.

first   second   third   fourth   fifth

Fractions

Now your child learns how to divide one thing into smaller parts. Fractions are placed here in the sequence, but children can usually start working with fractions once they are doing multiplication.

One easy way to introduce fractions is when cutting food, as above with a banana. Point out that you start with **one** banana. Cut it into two fairly equal pieces, and say, *"Each piece is one half."* Have your child count the pieces as one half and one half. Say, *"There are two halves."* Push the two halves together and say, *"One half plus one half equals one banana."*

Make four equal size pieces and say, *"There are four quarters."* Push the quarters back together and say, *"Four quarters equals one banana"*. Repeat this when cutting apples, celery, pieces of cheese, etc.

Good **iPad fractions apps** include **Pizza Fractions**, **Fractions App by Tap To Learn**, and **Match the Fraction**.

Montessori Print Shop has a beautiful printable material called **Fractions Cards and Labels** that are perfect for teaching fractions.

Other sources of nice, free fractions materials can be found at:

math-drills.com/fractions.shtml

math-aids.com/Fractions/Fractions_Lesson_Plan.html

helpingwithmath.com/printables/worksheets/fractions/fra0401identifying01.htm

"Free choice is one of the highest of all the mental processes."
Maria Montessori

Telling Time

Once your child has an understanding of amounts and numerals 0-100, she can learn to do cool things, like telling time. It helps to go step by step, building towards a real understanding of time and the clock.

Battery powered analog clocks (left), are available at office supply stores. They make it easy to see the minute marks, numerals, and the hands. Put a clock like this on the wall in your child's room.

Start with **seconds**. With your child, count the clicks of the **second hand**, starting at 12:00 and going once around the clock. Explore what you can do in one second, such as clap your hands, say your names fast, clap once each second, etc.

Tell your child that 60 seconds, or one time around the clock for the second hand, is **one minute**. Watch to see how the **minute hand** moves one click each time the second hand goes all the way around. *"There are 60 seconds in one minute."* Explore things you can do in one minute, like walking around the house, load the dishwasher, wash and dry your hands, etc.

Ask your child, *"How many minutes are there around the clock?"* Help only as needed and have your child count all the marks, starting at 12:00. Point out that 60 minutes, or one trip around for the minute hand, is **one hour**. Show your child the **hour hand**.

Wait for the time to reach the start of a new hour, or set the clock to read, say, 2:00. Tell your child that you two will check back and see how long an hour is. Watch TV, play a game, or do another activity, and see how much time has elapsed. All these activities will help your child get a sense of the passage of time. This seems obvious to us because we have lived according to the clock for years. It is not so with a young child, whose concepts of time are quite different from ours.

After these experiences, you can work on reading the time. Start with exact hours. Set the clock at each hour in sequence: 1:00, 2:00, 3:00, 4:00, etc., and have your child read the hours all the way to 12:00. Next, mix different hours. Sett the clock at 1:00, 7:00, 9:00, 2:00, etc., and have your child read the hours.

The Clock Series printables from **Montessori Print Shop** will help your child learn to read the clock. Good **iPad apps** for learning to tell time include **Telling Time HD, Telling Time Free**, and **Telling Time the Easy Way**.

The **Big Time 12 Hr. Student Clock** from **Learning Resources** (left) is another excellent material for learning to tell time.

When your child can recognize and read the hours, start using the minute hand. Set the clock at 1:00. As you move the minute hand clockwise, have your child count off the minutes to 15. *"The clock now says 15 minutes after one o'clock."* Continue to 30 and 45 minutes after 1:00. Repeat starting with other hours for practice. Online worksheets to help your child learn to read the clock are available at:

homeschoolmath.net/worksheets/clock.php

enchantedlearning.com/time

Using a Calendar

One of the best ways to teach your child to learn to use a calendar is to hang a simple calendar with easy to read dates in your child's room and use it on a daily basis. You can spend a lot of time learning the days of the week, the months, etc., as separate activities, but using a real calendar day to day works really well. Once your child has been through a couple of years she will have it down pat for life. Be sure to write down special dates, appointments, and holidays so your child gets used to using the calendar as a planning tool. Online resources include:

enchantedlearning.com/wordwheels/themes/seasons

pre-kpages.com/calendars

mrsjonesroom.com/teachers/calendars.html

Exchanging coins

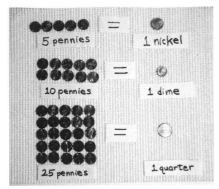

5 pennies = 1 nickel

10 pennies = 1 dime

25 pennies = 1 quarter

Get out 25 pennies, a nickel, a dime, and a quarter. Show your child that 5 pennies make one nickel, 10 pennies make one dime, and 25 pennies make one quarter. Lay out the coins and = sign cards to give your child a visual experience of these coin amounts.

Give your child 5, then 10, then 25 pennies and let her figure out to give you first a nickel, then a dime, and finally a quarter back. Then do it in reverse – give you child a nickel, dime and then a quarter and have your child give you the correct number of pennies back. Work on this until you feel your child understands these coins and the amounts they represent. Now try it with two nickels, then two dimes, then two quarters. Use the Hundred Board if needed to help your child figure things out. Keep playing this game, adding more nickels, dimes, and quarters as your child gets more comfortable. **Splash Money** is an excellent iPad app for teaching about money.

Making a dollar

Children love to use bills! Get the **Hundred Board** you used earlier (p. 140). Have your child lay out 100 pennies and count them as she goes. Now, place an = sign to the right of the board, and a dollar bill to the right of that. "*100 pennies makes one dollar.*"

Have your child count again, stopping at every fifth penny and placing a nickel there. There should be 20 nickels on the board at the end. "*Twenty nickels make one dollar.*" Repeat, except using dimes. "*Ten dimes makes one dollar.*" Repeat, using 4 quarters. "*Four quarters makes one dollar.*"

Practice exchanging these coins for dollar bills. When your child is familiar with making one dollar, use two dollars, etc.

Buy & sell

A toy cash register, like the Learning Resources Pretend and Play in the photo, makes an excellent material for learning about money. Let your child organize the toy money in the drawers and practice with him, buying and selling various items. Good blog posts about money are:

educationofours.blogspot.com/2012/04/money-exchange-game.html

countingcoconuts.blogspot.com/2011/06/money-matters-intro-to-money-shopping.html

carrotsareorange.com/teaching-kids-money-steps/#comment-1533

carrotsareorange.com/13880/

App Toy – Cash Register is a fun and educational iPad app.

A piggy bank is wonderful for learning about saving money. Your child can save for something specific he wants to buy, as well as start a bank account. It is also fun to go to a coin exchange machine when the bank is full.

Money games

Good games involving money include **Monopoly Jr.**, **PayDay**, **Money Bags**, and **Moneywise Kids**.

Measurement

When you need to measure something, introduce your child to the ruler. Use a 12" ruler. Show her the markings that stand for inches and have her count how many inches there are in one foot. Measuring and marking your child's height on a door frame is always great.

She can now go through the house measuring things if she likes. A list of objects and how long they are makes a good sight word reading activity.

When your child measures something that is between two inch marks in length, you can show him the half and quarter inch marks. If you haven't already, this is a good time to introduce **Fractions** (p. 146).

Get your child a small tape measure. Let him measure things. Introduce the terms length, height, and width; and show her the numbers on the tape measure. Cut pipe cleaners different lengths, like 1", 2", 5", etc., and let your child measure and sort them by length. Once he has done this awhile, have a contest where you two estimate how long, high, or wide things are and win prizes for the closest answer.

Weigh, measure, estimate

When your child has some experience with measuring lengths of objects, have him estimate how long something is just by looking at it, and then check with the ruler to see how close he came. Use a simple **postal scale** to introduce weighing objects. Have your child help you weigh fruits and vegetables at the store.

Using cups your child cannot see through, pour measured amounts of water into each - 1 oz., 3 oz., 5 oz., etc. Let your child hold the cups to compare their weights and line them up from lightest to heaviest going left to right. Have her pour each, one at a time, into a measuring cup, and read how many ounces each glass contains to see if she graded them correctly.

Do the activity above using salt or small beans and measuring them out with a tablespoon. Put 1, 2, and 3 tablespoons into the cups and let your child weigh and compare them as above. She can scoop the material back out using a tablespoon to check.

> *"The child builds his inmost self out of the deeply held impressions he receives."*
>
> **Maria Montessori**

Writing & Reading

Practical Life and **Sensorial** materials prepare a child for math, writing, and reading. The hand and finger muscle control these materials develop help a child execute a **writing grasp**. Children learn to concentrate, and are exposed to words on labels and cards. The Sensorial materials help a child focus on line and form, arranging objects from left to right, and using graphic printed materials. With sufficient opportunities to work with Practical Life and Sensorial materials, learning math, writing, and reading is natural and stress-free.

Children usually enter a **Sensitive Period for reading and writing around age four**. If we take advantage of this time of increased interest and ability, children surprise us with how fast they learn. Many children struggle with reading because they start too late. Most children eventually do fine. Many more could be excellent readers with high comprehension and a love of reading much earlier, with less effort and more joy. The simple sequence of activities and materials shown here will guide you in teaching your child to write and read.

If you have not invested in an **iPad** or **iPad Mini** yet, now would be a great time. The many excellent reading and writing apps recommended in the following pages allow children to learn almost everything they need to know just by using them. Once a child can identify abstract symbols, digital apps are a natural and really fun way to learn to read.

Learning to write

Young children typically learn to write before they learn to read, so let's do writing first. A child needs to be able to execute a proper writing grasp. This happens as a child uses the Practical Life materials, especially the **Transfer** activities (p. 59-60). Make sure your child has many opportunities to use these materials.

A **writing grasp** (left above) has the writing instrument held between the thumb and first finger in a pincer grip, while the other fingers curl underneath for support. If your child needs more help to do this, a device like the attachment shown at right above, from **Draw Your World**, can help as a temporary aid. In addition to Practical Life materials, **drawing** and **tracing** are excellent activities for practicing and developing a writing grasp. Keep drawing supplies like colored pencils, markers, crayons, scissors, and various kinds of paper available at all times in your child's room. Encourage your child to draw and color whenever she likes.

For tracing, crafts stores have wooden shapes and letters. Embroidery hoops, and plastic cookie cutters. The **Primary Shapes Template Set** (left) from **Learning Resources** is excellent. Encourage tracing as well as drawing, as both develop a writing grasp and an appreciation of line and form.

Once your child is developing a writing grasp, get a set of **Montessori Sandpaper Letters** in block style, lower case (left). These cost around $26 at Montessori Outlet, and will serve double duty for teaching your child the Phonetic Alphabet in just a bit. See page 157.

A shallow pan with a thin layer of cornmeal (left) works well for letter and numeral tracing practice. Your child can work at tracing the letter or number, and shake the pan to erase it. Have your child use one or two fingers.

 There are many good **iPad apps** for learning to write letters, including **Montessori Letter Sounds**, **Write On**, **Approach To Montessori: Numbers**, and **Letter School**. Get your child a stylus like the **Mini Alloy Stylus** shown at left. Encourage your child to use the stylus instead of his finger when writing.

Introduce the Montessori Sandpaper Letters by teaching your child the **Phonetic Alphabet** as shown starting on page 157. As your child learns the letter sounds, she can also be practicing writing them. Worksheets help, and you can find good free writing practice worksheets online at:

donnayoung.org/penmanship/k_1.htm

donnayoung.org/penmanship/zb-handwriting-animations.htm

handwritingworksheets.com/flash/printdots/index.htm

kidslearningstation.com

From this point on, learning to write letters and numerals is a matter of frequent practice.

Learning to Read

The most important thing you can do to help your child learn to read is to **read with your child every day**. Being read to regularly as a child is the factor that most highly predicts a child's success in learning to read. Let your child pick books he likes and read them with him every day. As you read, incorporate these tips:

Make reading time special. Sit close and cuddle. Make reading a warm, loving experience for your child. **Be animated and enthusiastic**. Use different voices for the characters and act excited and amazed by the story. **Encourage your child's participation**. Ask her what she thinks will happen next, who her favorite characters are, and what she is feeling while reading. **Draw your child's attention to the print**. Point out words and let your child read them. Let him try to read if he wants to. **Read from a variety of sources**, like magazines, signs, labels, etc.

Materials that promote reading skills

Many great printable materials from **Montessori Print Shop** help children build the visual skills required for reading, including:

Superimposed Geometric Figures	**Patterning Cards**
Three Part Cards (many kinds)	**What Does Not Belong?**
Phonics Sound & Picture Sorting	**Alphabet Cards**

Good iPad apps for developing reading skills include **Touch & Learn – Emotions, Labyrinth, Touch & Learn – ABC Alphabet and 123 Numbers, Little Patterns Shapes, A Preschool Pattern Recognition Game, Wood Puzzle Slider**, and **123 Domino.** Have your child use the stylus when working with these apps.

The Three Step Reading Sequence

Once your child starts showing spontaneous interest in words, the three step sequence shown here will help you teach her to read in the shortest possible time. Reading is a process of **decoding** symbols and learning to read **fluently.** The three steps are:

1. Phonics

Language is a code, and your child learns to break the code by learning one sound for each letter of the alphabet, called the **Phonetic Alphabet.** Using these sounds, your child practices **building phonetic words.** Finally, your child reads his first books using **phonetic readers.** This major achievement is a springboard for moving into step two. A preoccupation with phonics as a teaching tool after this point, while somewhat valuable, can actually hold a child back from progressing on in learning to read.

2. Sight Words

In the second step, your child learns to recognize the most common words when he sees them. Soon, your child will build and read sentences, and then start reading early reading books. The sight word process continues on for years as your child's sight word vocabulary grows.

3. **Reading**

Nothing builds reading skill like reading. While building a sight word vocabulary, your child can read early reader books on a daily basis. The goals are to promote fluent reading and a lifelong reading habit.

Step One: Phonics

Using the **Montessori Sandpaper Letters** (p. 153), teach your child the phonetic sound of each letter. This is the Phonetic Alphabet:

a	As in apple	n	As in nut
b	As in bat	o	As in off (sounds like 'aw')
c	As in cat	p	As in pet
d	As in dog	q	As in quit (sounds like 'qw')
e	As in elephant	r	As in red
f	As in fog	s	As in sit
g	As in gum	t	As in top
h	As in hat	u	As in up (sounds like 'uh')
i	As in if	v	As in victory
j	As in jet	w	As in wet
k	As in Kentucky	x	As in box (sounds like 'ks')
l	As in lap	y	As in yellow
m	As in mat	z	As in zoo

The vowels make their short vowel sounds. The consonants make their individual sounds. **Remember not to add an 'uh' sound after the consonants.** B just says 'b', as in boat, not 'buh'.

Start with the letters **m**, **a** and **t**. Do **Three Step Lessons** (p. 35) to teach your child the sounds of these letters, *not* the letter names. Once your child knows these three sounds, teach the rest, three at a time using Three Step Lessons, in this sequence:

u b c s o h g r e n p i f j l d v w y z x k q

As your child learns these letter sounds, introduce pictures of objects whose names start with the sounds. The **Phonics Sounds and Picture Sorting** printables from **Montessori Print Shop** are perfect for this. You can also search for images on objects online and use those. Free picture cards can be found at:

resources.sparkleplus.co.uk/sb370.pdf

page.reallygoodstuff.com/pdfs/301712.pdf

galacticphonics.com/cvc/resources/cvcpics.pdf

thehelpfulgarden.blogspot.com/2011/10/beginning-letter-sound-word-walls.html

Associating the letter sounds with the first sound in the names of the printed objects is an important step, don't leave it out! Good **iPad apps** for reinforcing and learning letter sounds include **Bitsboard**, **Starfall ABC's**, **Phonics Consonants Free**, **ABC Read Write Phonics**, and **Little Reader Three Letter Words**.

Word Building

Once your child knows the sounds through **h**, he can build phonetic words, in which each letter says its phonetic sound. These are also called **CVC words**, because they contain a Consonant – Vowel – Consonant.

Start with **cat**. Lay out the three letter sounds. Say "*Cat*" and emphasize the **c** sound. Ask your child to find that sound and lay it to the left. Say "*Cat*" again, emphasizing the **a** sound. Have your child find the **a** and set it to the right of the **c**. Say "*Cat*" again, emphasizing the **t** sound. Have your child set it to the right of the **a**. Point to and say each sound in rapid sequence: "**c,a,t**".

Now say the word while running your finger left to right over the letters: "*Cat*". Have your child say the sounds rapidly together to say the word. You and your child just built a word! This is a big deal, so make a fuss over it. Your child is now on the road to reading. Over a period of time, encourage your child to practice building lots of CVC words, such as:

cat	can	cub	bug	bun	bat
sun	mug	rug	tub	hat	map
hen	nut	pot	net	pan	cab
mop	hog	pen	ten	cap	pug

Find more CVC words online here:

3dinosaurs.com/printables/learningtoread/wordfamily.php

itsybitsylearners.com/abcs-123s/cvc-words

When your child has some skill building these words, introduce larger phonetic words, such as:

must	grab	trot	flop	slip	band	west
dust	blast	crop	soft	stamp	split	crisp
hasp	past	frog	cost	sand	drink	best
plan	last	camp	plastic	swim	frantic	trip
drag	snap	stand	blend	pond	glob	lips
cramp	trap	hand	lamp	flag	bank	stab
stub	mend	bend	send	tent	swept	crept
slept	link	milk	drip	gift	mist	wink
twist	frost	pond	drop	stop	cost	strip
melt	spend	bunk	skunk	trunk	drum	plum

Excellent **iPad apps** for word building include **Montessori Crosswords**, **ABC Spelling Magic Short Vowel Sounds**, **ABC Spelling Magic 2**, **Bitsboard**, **ABC Pocket Phonics**, and **Phonics Make A Word**. These apps let your child practice whenever he wants and provide the practice necessary to master word building skills. It is possible today for a child to learn to read using only iPad apps!

Reading Phonetic Readers

The final part of the Phonics step is to have your child read books that use all, or mostly, phonetic words. There are many choices, including:

Starfall Short Vowel Pals and **Learn To Read** books (starfall.com)

The Bob Books (Amazon)

Miss Rhonda's Readers (missrhondasreaders.com)

Starfall has an entire learn to read program free on their wonderful site, just follow the numbered steps. You can find free downloadable phonetic readers at **freephoneticreaders.com**

Read with your child at first, encouraging her to sound out words as needed and to gradually start reading on her own. Independent reading of these books is the goal. When your child has had **plenty of practice** reading these books and building phonetic words, it is time to move to step two: **Sight Words**.

Step Two: Sight Words

Using phonics, your child has had a successful introduction to written language. Now it is time to start building a vocabulary of sight words, because we read by recognizing words when we see them. This is a process of practice and memorization, so different kinds of activities are used to add variety and maintain enthusiasm. Goals for step two are for your child to be able to:

Recognize and read 300-1000 sight words

Learn to combine these words into sentences

Start reading early reader books.

iPad apps shine when it comes to learning sight words. Great apps include **Bitsboard, Fry Words, Abby Sight Words, Little Reader Four Letter Words, Sight Words 1-300: Kids Learn** (a fabulous app), and **ABC Phonics Word Family Writing**. It is hard to imagine better resources for a child to work with to learn sight words and have fun.

There is an eBook on iBooks that shows you exactly what apps to buy and how to use them all in sequence to teach your child to read: **Teach Your Preschooler To Read Using the iPad**.

The Dolch and Fry Words

The Dolch and Fry words are collections of the most common words seen in print. These make the logical first sight words for children to learn. Great resources for these word lists and activities can be found at:

kidzone.ws/dolch/index.htm

dolchword.net

mrsperkins.com/dolch.htm

The Funny Dolch Word Books (Amazon)

classroom.jc-schools.net/waltkek/Sight%20Word%20Resources.html

mie.democratandchronicle.com/sites/default/files/documents/Frys_Sight_Words.pdf

Scholastic has a great series of four sight word workbooks available on Amazon, titled:

25 Read and Write Mini-Books

100 Write-and-Learn Sight Word Practice Pages

40 Sensational Sight Word Games

100 Sight Word Mini-Books

Make up flash cards, play memory games (p. 89), tape sight words up in your child's room, and encourage your child to use the workbooks and iPad apps listed here repeatedly over a good period of time to learn many sight words.

When your child has learned a good number of sight words, he can use them to make sentences. Excellent **iPad apps** for this include **Sentence Maker** and **Sentence Builder**. You can also print out individual words onto cards, lay them out at random, and then give your child sentences to make. She finds the words and lays them out in order left to right.

More good online sight word resources can be found at:

1plus1plus1equals1.com/YouCanRead.html

quiz-tree.com/Sight-Words_main.html

bingocardcreator.com/dolch-sight-words-bingo.htm

wordsearchcreator.org

The final piece in step two is to give your child **early reader books** that use mostly the common sight words she has been learning. Examples include:

Brand New Readers (Amazon)

carolhurst.com/profsubjects/reading/emergentreaders.html

Level One Readers (Scholastic, Amazon)

usborne.com/veryfirstreading/books/books.aspx

Miss Rhonda's First Readers, Sets 2 & 3

icanread.com

Read Me Stories – Children's Books (iPad app)

Dr. Seuss Beginner Collection #1 (iPad app)

Step Three: Reading

Over a good period of time, your child has learned to break the code of language, build words, make sentences, recognize many words on sight, and read his first books on his own. From here on, **nothing builds reading skill like reading**. Follow your child's interests and let her pick out books to read. Children learn to read much faster and easier when they are reading a book they are personally very interested in. If your child finds a word he does not know, teach him to simply ask you what it says. Tell him and let him continue reading.

If you see your child having trouble reading, the most likely cause is going through the first two steps of the process too quickly, without sufficient opportunities for practice. Reading is a lot like math. Each step must be mastered before moving on for a child to truly understand and use these skills. Go back and help your child fill in any gaps.

Good Books for New Readers

Books highly recommended for new readers include:

Kipper's A to Z: An Alphabet Adventure
The Icky Bug Alphabet Book
Eating the Alphabet
Brown Bear, Brown Bear, What Do You See?
Bubble Trouble
You Read To Me, I'll Read To You: Very Short Stories To Read Together
Good Luck Bear
Thank you Bear
Why Mosquitoes Buzz In People's Ears
Where's Spot
Spot's First Words
Rosie's Walk
Spot Goes To School
Have You Seen My Cat?
My Mother Is Mine
Goodnight Dog
Hop On Pop
Green Eggs and Ham
Are You My Mother?
The Cat In The Hat
Horton Hears a Who
How the Grinch Stole Christmas
The Snowy Day
Alexander and the Terrible, Horrible, No Good Very Bad Day
The Rose In My Garden
Blueberries For Sal
The Napping House
All The World
My Garden
The Giving Tree
The Big Dipper
Boo Hoo Bird
Bringing the Rain to Kapiti Plain
Terrific
At Night
Every Friday
One is a Snail, Ten is a Crab: A Counting by Feet Book
Where the Wild Things Are
The 'How Do Dinosaurs' series
Today and Today

Curious George
Leo The Late Bloomer
Gregory, The Terrible Eater
The Day Jimmy's Boa Ate The Wash
The Ball Bounced
Animals Should Definitely Not Wear Clothing
The Jacket I Wear In the Snow
Drummer Hoff
Hattie and the Fox

Good first iPad eBooks

Bookboard
Dr. Seuss Beginner Book Collection #1
MeeGenius! Kid's Books
14 Best of the Best preschooler's books for iPad
Booksy Learn To Read Books
Scholastic eBooks
The Oceanhouse Media Collection Check out the Magic School Bus eBooks
Disney Digital Books
Good Night Moon
Rounds: Parker Penguin
Rounds: Franklin Frog
The Chalk Box Story
Sleepy Mole's Moving Day
Five Little Monkeys Jumping On The Bed
How Rocket Learned to Read
Bella Goes Bump In The Night
Mouse and Owl Check out School Zone's Start To Read! series

Good first Android eBooks

Dr. Seuss Books (Google Play)
Dr. Seuss Books (Amazon)
Oceanhouse Media Books
Booksy Learn To Read Platform
MeeGenius! Childen's Books
iStoryBooks
Read Me Stories
Just Grandma and Me
Good Night Moon

The Going to Bed Book
Ant and Grasshopper 3D
Good Night Train
The Grumpy Family
Grandpa Grumpy's Family

Making your own books

Children love to read about themselves and events that impact their lives. Making homemade books together is a wonderful activity, and will produce books that are very meaningful to your child. Children often read these books again and again, which is what you want when a child is learning to read.

Homemade books are not hard to create. Keep supplies on hand: glue sticks, computer printer, paper, and a stapler. Put a sheet of colored construction paper on top of a few sheets of white paper, fold in half, staple along the fold, and you have a book. You can also punch holes in two card stock sheets for the covers and along one side of the pages and tie the book together with yarn. Another good method of making books can be found at:

premeditatedleftovers.com/easy-and-inexpensive-homemade-book-to-make-with-your-child

Watch the video here: **youtube.com/watch?v=N7zudZYVSGw**

When your child is writing, she can write the text for her books herself. Until then, have her dictate what to write and write it in yourself using block letters, like the style the sandpaper letters are made in. If you do the text on a word processor, use **Century Gothic** type, like the sandpaper letters. Print photos and glue them into the book. Homemade books are wonderful early readers, precious memories, even gifts.

When your child has a memorable experience, takes a trip, even has a remarkable dream, make a book about it! Anything that is meaningful to your child can provide the raw material for a book. Use your child's own words on the pages. Include your child's drawings as well as photos.

Good **iPad apps** for creating books are **Scribblepress, My Story, Book Press**, and **Story Patch**. You can paste in photos, publish eBooks online, and do all kinds of creative things with these apps. This is the future of books, and these apps allow your child to gain invaluable experience working with eBooks and producing his own books.

Improving Comprehension

Reading is only part of the story. Children also have to develop good comprehension skills: the abilities to retain and understand what they read. It is easy to encourage preschoolers to improve their comprehension skills simply by talking about what they read.

Before you read, talk about the story. If it is a new book, flip through the pages and talk about that you see. If it is a book your child has read before, talk about the characters, what happens, and your child's favorite parts of the story. **During** reading, talk about the story, the characters, and ask your child what he thinks will happen next. **After** reading, talk about the plot, what happens to the characters, and what your child liked or did not like about the story. All this conversation about books will help your child focus attention and learn to retain what she reads.

Encourage your child to continue reading every day. Many children now rely largely on video and other image-based internet content for their information. Spend time each day reading.

"Children are human beings to whom respect is due, superior to us by reason of their innocence and of the greater possibilities of their future."

"It is the child who makes the man, and no man exists who was not made by the child he once was."

Maria Montessori

Parting Note

I hope the activities in this book provide your child with many wonderful, brain building experiences. The most important results of early learning are not advanced skills in math and reading. The real goals are improved brain architecture, a positive and confident self-image, and a true love of learning.

Helping a young child build better brain architecture, and watching the process happen, is incredibly rewarding. If you decide to homeschool, you can continue the process without missing a beat. If your child heads off to school, I encourage you to maintain an atmosphere of learning and discovery at home while you support your child's school and get involved in what is happening there. Once a child starts school, many parents think education only happens there. This is not so! Continue exposing your child to many different experiences in the arts and sciences. Meet and talk to all kinds of people. Take trips to interesting places and learn everything you can. Pursue hobbies, join clubs. Get out in nature regularly and explore with your child. The more a child is exposed to, the greater the child's understanding of the world and the better the chance that the child will find a field of great interest to pursue as an adult.

More quotes from Maria Montessori

"The more the capacity to concentrate is developed, the more often the profound tranquility in work is achieved, the clearer will be the manifestation of discipline within the child."

"It is almost possible to say that there is a mathematical relationship between the beauty of his surroundings and the activity of the child; he will make discoveries rather more voluntarily in a gracious setting than in an ugly one."

"We must, therefore, quit our roles as jailers and instead take care to prepare an environment in which we do as little as possible to exhaust the child with our surveillance and instruction."

"No one can be free unless he is independent: therefore, the first, active manifestations of the child's individual liberty must be so guided that through this activity he may arrive at independence. We habitually serve children; and this is not only an act of servility toward them, but it is dangerous, since it tends to suffocate their useful, spontaneous activity."

"The lesson must be presented in such a way that the personality of the teacher shall disappear. There shall remain in evidence only the object to which she wishes to call the attention of the child."

"The teacher's task is not to talk, but to prepare and arrange a series of motives for activity in a special environment made for the child."

"We then found that individual activity is the one factor that stimulates and produces development, and that this is not truer for the little ones of preschool age than it is for upper school children."

"The role of education is to interest the child profoundly in an external activity to which he will give all of his potential. Education is not something which the teacher does. It is a natural process which develops spontaneously."

"There is no description, no image in any book that is capable of replacing the sight of real trees, and all of the life to be found around them in a real forest. How often is the soul of man - especially in childhood - deprived because he is not allowed to come in contact with nature?"

"Our aim is not only to make the child understand, and still less to force him to memorize, but so to touch his imagination as to enthuse him to his innermost core."

"Education starts at birth."

"The essential thing is to arouse such an interest that it engages the child's whole personality."

Made in the USA
Middletown, DE
09 January 2015